Act Like A Man

A Collection of Plays Starring The Average Adult Male

By

Jeremey W. Gingrich

ISBN: 1-4140-0124-X (e-book)
ISBN: 1-4140-0125-8 (Paperback)
ISBN: 1-4140-0123-1 (Dust Jacket)

Library of Congress Control Number: 2003112393

This book is printed on acid free paper.

Printed in the United States of America
Bloomington, IN

1stBooks rev. – 11/07/03

I'd like to dedicate this work my parents, Frank and Connie, who raised me in an environment that fostered a creative imagination, facilitated by love. And, because if I didn't, I'm sure I would become the unfortunate victim of some gruesome "accident."

I'd also like to thank my good friend Jeff, without whom this book would never have happened. Everyone should be so lucky as to have such a friend.

Table of Contents

Introduction

I recently discovered that my father's favorite movie of all time is "The Godfather." Since that discovery I have seen the movie eighteen times. One of my favorite parts occurs at the beginning, when the singer Johnny Fontaine, a thinly veiled Frank Sinatra character, comes to Don Corleone and asks for help in getting into a movie. As Fontaine begins to cry, whining, "What can I do," the Godfather grabs his arms and starts shaking him violently, yelling "You can act like a man!" Of course, "The Godfather" is a very masculine movie, so such comments can be dismissed as par for the course in the stereotypical, macho, Italian gangster movie. However, as I watched these important men, Vito and Michael, making important decisions, though mostly illegal and murderous, I felt very inadequate. After all, I couldn't fathom making a decision of that caliber, and if those are the kinds of decisions that men make…real men…and I can't make them…then what does that make me?

Now, I'm not suggesting we all compare our life decisions to Michael Corleone's decision to kill the heads of the Five Families. I am merely saying that, to me, a decisive act of conviction and confidence comes as easy as Chinese "Wheel of Fortune." And that lack of conviction, from time to time, makes me feel incredibly insufficient. An example of such inadequacy can be seen in a recent incident at a KFC, formerly a Kentucky Fried Chicken before the country developed a deathly fear of the word "fried." A couple ordered their food right before me and then went to sit down at a booth with their backs to the counter. After I ordered my food, I merely waited at the counter for it to be prepared. While I waited there, the couple's food was finished and placed on the counter, and the worker bee behind the counter called out their number, but they were engrossed in conversation and didn't hear. The employee called out their number again, but again they weren't listening. So, as I stood there, waiting for my food with nothing to do, I was struck with a moment of altruistic service to my fellow man. I thought maybe I could take the tray of food over to the couple, since they seemed to be otherwise engaged. The problem was, one of their meals was on an open plate, with the food exposed, and I wasn't sure if this couple would feel uneasy about a total stranger handing them their plate of vulnerable food. I was also afraid of simply walking up to the couple and telling them that their food was ready. I thought if I did this, they would think I was some pompous asshole who thought of himself as too important to carry the tray over to them. So, what did I do? I stood there quietly debating my options, not moving an inch, even when my food came. And as I just stood there, having this internal argument, the young employee behind the counter came back from around the counter and handed the tray to the couple personally.

This pathetic display of indecisiveness was followed with another pathetic display of righteousness. As a method of validating my lack of action, I began to disparage the people whose food was the object of conflict. "Why weren't they paying attention?" I asked myself. "Did they not think their food was ever going to be ready?" These were the thoughts that occurred to me to justify my immobile state during the whole fiasco. But as I examined past experiences I've had concerning such situational ambiguity, I realize I've always either made bad decisions or no decision at all. This revelation had the potential to become a depressing discovery, because after all, if I can't handle a simple decision at a KFC, how am I going to handle the decisions concerning major policy at a job, or the more frightening issues concerning the permanent institutions of marriage and parenthood? However, instead of succumbing to an enveloping depression, I started observing other men in similar situations, to see how I behaved in comparison to them. And after some study and observation, I've discovered the simple truth that most of us are simply bumbling around with no real clue as to how to handle anything.

I've come to believe this is why the great men in history are so revered. It is seen as a miracle that an average man, the regular Joe that puts his pants on one leg at a time like all the rest of us, could rise to the ranks of a Franklin Roosevelt, or a General MacArthur, or a George Washington Carver (I'm a big peanut-butter fan). This could also be why action movies are so admired by the male population. When Clint Eastwood or Bruce Willis jumps off a building or shoots some scumbag in the face, they are worshiped for their decisiveness and quick action. However, the fact is, in both fictional and non-fictional cases, these are not average men. The average man is the man you meet every day: The man trying to pass his fourteen-year-old son off as eleven to get a cheaper movie ticket; the man yelling out of his car window at somebody who's just cut him off, but who, ten minutes later, cuts somebody off himself; and the man complaining about his failed relationships, all the while working diligently to screw them all up. These are the "average" men…living lives wrought with insecurity, ambiguity and immaturity, and yet, somehow, having the time of their lives.

These are the qualities I have placed in the characters of these plays. They are all thoroughly flawed, but also somehow likeable in their enjoyment of their flaws. They are seemingly intelligent people, and yet they have lived in society for so long and have no real clue as to how to behave when confronted by life questions, the most extreme of these questions being the search for a person of the opposite sex with whom to share their lives. It is revealed in the first short scene how ridiculous men can be when reacting to the finality of marriage and monogamy, and that insecurity with permanence is expounded upon in the other characters, not just in marriage and family but in all aspects of living.

I have auditioned for plays before, and I've even been fortunate enough to get some decent roles. Throughout the process, however, I have found it near impossible to relate to some of the characters. Now, part of this can be attributed to my limited capacity for abstract thought. However, most of my associative inability is due to the fact that I typically do not act with the conviction and resolve that most characters do in the typical play. This is why I have laced the characters in the following plays with faults and limitations. I want actors to get a hold of these plays and have fun with that insecurity and fear. I want the average guy to read these scripts and fight for these roles because they can see themselves having some real fun with them…all the while just being themselves.

Finally, it is important to me that people who read these plays do not think that I live my life the way these characters do, and that I hate myself for it. Though I do live my life as most of these characters, I love my life and the way I live it. I complain about my shortcomings on a daily basis, but I laugh hysterically whenever they make an appearance. The thing that's most important, and is prevalent in almost every piece of my work, is the necessity of a close-knit group of similar men, whom we call our friends, or even just one friend, that sticks with you not only in spite of all the insecurities, not only in spite of all the imperfections, but because of them. Because, though the average man may live a life wrought with misery, that misery loves company. And while Don Corleone would never label our behavior as "acting like a man," I feel confident, through my years of study and erudition, that we are still acting like the "average man." And that's good enough for me. Enjoy.

Symbolic Relations

A One-Scene Short

Jeremey W. Gingrich

<u>Symbolic Relations</u>

Pete is a bachelor with a problem. He has a live-in girlfriend, Morgan, who has grown tired of simply being a roommate with sexual benefits. On the day that she has this epiphany, Pete has to think fast to maintain his status quo, the life that he has become accustomed to, and would prefer to continue. This short scene can work as an instructional video for the men who find themselves in similar situations, but more than that, it is a testimonial in denial of the belief that "the truth will set you free."

Time: The Present

SCENE - *This all takes place in a small, two-bedroom apartment, where the living room is the focus of attention. There is a couch center stage, with a coffee table and a little chair with an ottoman stage left. There is a little table next to the front door, for keys and change and such. The upstage portion is the corridor to the other rooms, to include the kitchen and the bedroom. Sitting on the couch is our hero, PETE, dressed in jogging pants, a dirty T-shirt, Homer Simpson slippers, and a ratty old robe. There are shorts, a* *sweaty T-shirt and basketball shoes scattered on the floor. PETE is holding a remote control and clicking it towards a television set stage right. PETE's girlfriend, MORGAN, has been out shopping, and will return shortly. PETE possesses the ability to talk to the audience, which he uses often.*

PETE

(After a few clicks of the remote, he gets up, throws the remote on the couch, looks at his watch, and then talks to the audience.)

I find it amazing how I can sit in front of a television set for three hours and not recall a single thing that I have watched. Everything seems to run together...and it's all crap! I was at a coffee shop this morning and a couple sitting next to me actually had a twenty minute conversation on the "Survivor" competition, and it was of a serious nature. I seriously overheard them arguing, passionately arguing, over who they would've voted off the island and why. Are these the kinds of questions television was meant to inspire? No! I remember when primetime was ruled by serious, thought-provoking dramas like "St. Elsewhere" and "Hill Street Blues." I can remember when the nightly entertainment included comedies like "Cheers" and "The Cosby Show." That was interesting, entertaining television. Now, reality TV has the American public watching grown men and women eating sheep intestines and various insects as the current form of entertainment. I used to worship television as a God, to whom I've sacrificed most of my young life. Now, I want to punch myself in the face for knowing who won the first "American Idol."

(He walks back to the couch and sits, flipping the remote as he talks. After a pause.)

Morgan loves "American Idol," and she makes me watch it with her...and I have to be dead quiet while she watches it, despite all the disparaging remarks I wish to make. She's a great girl, but this reality TV thing has to stop. Hopefully it's just a phase she's going through, like rap music for me when I was in high school. But hell, give me Snoop Dogg over "Fear Factor" any day. Morgan and I have been living together for ten months now, and I'm pretty proud of myself. I've typically always been very temporary about myself…constantly changing moods, likes and dislikes…so I figured I'd never be able to settle down with just one woman, and yet here we sit. This reeks of maturity.

(His eye has caught something on television.)
Oooh, Looney Tunes!

(He turns up the television, so we hear Looney Tunes cartoon sounds. MORGAN walks in carrying bags. She has a grocery bag and a JCPenny shopping bag. She is wearing jeans and a nice sweater, black boots and a black leather jacket.)

MORGAN

There's my always-productive man-about—town. Looking quite debonair, Mr. Bond.

(She sees what's on television.)
Oh, and educational programming I see…

PETE

Hush, woman! This is a Daffy Duck classic.

MORGAN

(She grabs the remote out of his hands and turns the TV off with plenty of attitude.)
Oh, no. You did not just "Hush" me!

PETE

(After looking at her for a second.)
You know, when you wear your leather jacket, you begin to take on the attitude of a trailer park Jerry Springer guest, did I ever tell you that?

(He mocks her voice with excess attitude, and he snaps his fingers in the air.)
"Oh, no you didn't!"

(He laughs. She just smiles.)
Come here, girl. Give us a kiss.
MORGAN
In that outfit, no thanks. I know how long it's been
since that robe's been washed.
*(She takes the groceries to the kitchen, drops the bags
off, but leaves the shopping bags next to the coffee
table.)*
Have you even changed out of that thing all day? Oh,
sorry. I should revise. Have you moved from that spot
all day?

PETE
(Slightly offended.)
Yes...

MORGAN
(Looking down at the clothes on the floor.)
Oh, yes. I can see now. You evidently went to the gym
and left these clever clues for me to gather. Well, I'll
leave them for now.

PETE
Yeah, I got up and got some coffee in me, then went to
play ball down at the Y. There weren't too many
people there in the morning, so it was easy for me to
get a few games in.

MORGAN
You know, one of these days, you're going to have to
grasp the fact that you are 28 now, and no matter how
much you practice, or how much you play, you're not
making Varsity. Just succumb to your age and take up
golf or racquetball or something.
*(She walks back from the kitchen with a box of Krispy
saltine crackers.)*
Hey, you wanted Krispy saltines, right? That was the
brand I got.

PETE

Oh, Morgan. Jesus! No, not Krispy! I can only eat
Premium. Don't you know this about me by now?
What am I, a stranger?

MORGAN
(Snapping back at him.)

I'll give you a thousand dollars if you can tell me my
birthday!

PETE
(Changing the subject.)

So, what else did you buy?
(He starts looking through the shopping bag.)

MORGAN

Some underwear…and a scarf.

PETE
(Intrigued by the word "underwear.")

Oooh. Wait a minute…That's a JC Penny bag.

MORGAN

So?

PETE

Well, it's just that women have access to very sexy
stores for underwear…Victoria's Secret or Frederick's
of Hollywood…JC Penny underwear is kind
of…utilitarian, isn't it? Where's the sexy red and pink
stuff?

MORGAN

I happen to like shopping at Penny's, Pete! And by the
way, I had a great day, thanks for asking. Some people
couldn't spend all day sitting on their ass. So, I decided
to treat myself to new underwear, you'll excuse me if I
didn't ask your advice. I happened to get the advice of
a very nice gentleman in the store.

PETE

Baby, you know I needed this day off. Jesus, since
they've switched us to twelve-hour shifts down at the
bar, I've worked eight days straight. What gentleman?

                    MORGAN
You only worked eight days straight because you took
over Angelo's weekend shift so he could take his girl
to Baltimore.
                      PETE
Who the hell goes to Baltimore, anyway? And, please,
somebody call the Guinness Book of Records for this
historic day. A woman is complaining that her man is
being too much of a nice guy! Now, what gentleman
helped you with shopping?
                    MORGAN
Just some guy who saw me browsing in scarves and
asked to help. He said the blue in this scarf brought out
the color in my eyes.
                      PETE
Your eyes are blue?
                    MORGAN
Oh, you King of Romance.
                      PETE
Then what? Was this guy like a personal shopper or
something? Did he work at Penny's?
                    MORGAN
No, he just happened to be shopping there and asked if
he could help. His name was Stuart.
                      PETE
            (Piecing together the clues.)
Hmmm. Guy named Stuart…helps a woman pick out a
scarf…Okay, how was work then?
                    MORGAN
            (Sensing the implication.)
He happens to be extremely heterosexual, smartass! In
fact…I gave him my number. We're going out on
Tuesday.

                      PETE
            (With a slight laugh.)

You're going out…Excuse me…did you say you were going out…like on a date? What is this? What are you trying to tell me?

MORGAN

I'm telling you I'm tired of being your safety net, Pete. When you asked me to move in with you, I thought it was going to lead up to something. But then you had to be your typical funny self and say…and I'll never forget this…"It's like we'll be college roommates, but with lots of sex." And sure, I laughed when you said it. I always laugh. I can always be counted on for a laugh, can't I? But that's all I am to you, Peter. I'm your roommate for sex…and your audience. And I'm tired of it! So, since we're not moving forward, I've decided to move us backward. We're no longer exclusive, Pete. Go ahead! Unleash your troubled soul on all those women you've denied yourself…and don't you dare lie to me and tell me you haven't thought about them!

PETE

(Still taken by surprise by this whole conversation.)
What? Who "them"…What "them"?

MORGAN

I may not be a quick learner, Pete, but I do learn. Your sense of commitment is…

(She looks down at the clothes on the floor.)
Look at your clothes for Christ's sake!

PETE

What the hell do my clothes have to do with anything?

MORGAN

(She walks around the apartment picking up the clothes as she mentions them.)
Arizona shorts…St. John's shirt…Duke hats…a Syracuse jacket…Pete, you went to Cornell for three years! You never even applied to any of these schools!

PETE

(After looking at her in confusion, he talks slowly.)
What the hell…

9

MORGAN

It's symbolic damn it! You can't even decide on one team to root for, you think you can fool me into thinking you could be content with just one woman? These are symbols of your lack of commitment!

(She throws the clothes at him.)

You're not fooling anyone! And I am not oblivious, Peter, though you apparently think I am. I see you when we're out together. I see your head turn at every woman that passes by with even a little shake in her ass...

PETE

It's not my fault they shake their asses!

MORGAN

...And how do you think that makes me feel? Or do you even think about my feelings at all? Christ, Pete, my younger sister, four years younger, got married four months ago. I can't be wasting my time with some Peter Pan case.

(She fights back tears.)

I can't take your shit anymore!

PETE

Wait a minute! Just wait...

(He grabs her to calm her but she pulls away from him, which angers him more.)

Just sit down for a second, will you? I've got some things to say here and it might not be what you want to hear...but you got your shots in, so now it's my turn.

(She sits down.)

Now look, I'm not really sure what this all means, so let me try to replay it in my head. If I can grasp this correctly, you're telling me that you want to break up with me, date this Stuart guy, and still live in this apartment while I wait to "figure things out"? Is that right? No, baby, you're made of glass, okay! I see right through you! In all likelihood, there is no Stuart, but I'll give you the benefit of the doubt and say there is. If he does exist, you're only using him as an ultimatum to force my hand. You think you'll throw this little tantrum, threaten me with this Stuart, and I'll fall to my knees and propose to you right here and now. Well, I'm sorry to disappoint you, darling. Jesus, I'm supposed to trust you, Morgan! A relationship is based on trust and love…whatever that is. You see, I'm honest with you! I admit it! I don't know what love is! I don't try to trick you into pretending to love me. And yes, I do look at other women, and maybe that's wrong, I don't know, but I have never once even so much as asked another woman to coffee since you moved in here! I respected you enough to remain solely with you, despite which way my head moved from day to day!

MORGAN

(Upset.)

And how am I supposed to feel…

PETE

(Ignoring her, pacing, picking up some of his aforementioned clothes.)

And using my clothes as a symbol of a lack of commitment? What the hell was that, dime-store psychology?

(He throws the clothes on the floor. He then grabs the box of crackers, speaking sarcastically.)

But wait, I only like Premium crackers and no others. Is that a symbol of how I can commit? Oh and let's look at you for a second, shall we? I took a psychology class once, too. Hmmm? Why do you watch reality television? Could it be that you are unhappy with the reality you have created for yourself?

MORGAN

(Crying.)

Are you joking about this?

PETE

(Still rolling.)

11

And you think I don't remember your little sister's wedding? You wouldn't stop crying for three days! But if you let her life dictate what you do with your own, well then that's just psychotic and I'm glad we got that out in the open.

(MORGAN starts to cry harder, but PETE mocks her.)

Oh, boo hoo hoo, my clever plan to trick Pete into marrying me didn't work, boo hoo.

(Now his anger is rising.)

I can't believe you would do this, Morgan! Christ, I loved you!

MORGAN

(Scared at the past tense of the word, but not backing down.)

No, these are lies! You just loved the idea of a safety net...

PETE

(Very serious, almost growling in anger.)

No, God damn it, I loved you! I can see that now! I can see it now because what you said hurt me so much. Alright, I admit it. You caught me! I'm afraid! I'm scared to death of making the wrong decision! And maybe that's not the right way to live, but it is MY WAY, Morgan! This is the rest of our lives we're talking about! Yours and mine! I can screw up my life, no problem, but I was scared to death that after years of enduring my shit that I would screw up your life too, and that you would hate me for it. I couldn't live with that. But I could live with you.

(He's starting to tear up.)

And that's why I asked you to move in with me, and that's why I've spent the last ten months with you in what I assumed to be relative bliss. But now...the fact that you can try to force me into something you know I'm not ready for...simply means I did not know what kind of person you truly were.

12

(He tears up some more. MORGAN tries to get close to him to hug him but he violently pulls away and his tears flow faster.)
You want to hug somebody…hug your damn Stuart!
    (He stomps to the front door and opens it.)
Please get out!

MORGAN
No, Petey, please! Please, honey, I only did it because I love you! I was afraid, too, baby. I was scared and I just love you so much. Please, please, don't let it be over! I'm so sorry! I…

PETE
Please just leave. I need some time to myself.
    (MORGAN walks out the door and looks back to him as she walks.)

MORGAN
I'll be back in an hour. I'm really sorry, Pete. Please…
    (PETE closes the door. You can hear her sobbing on the other side of the door, though PETE's sobs are almost as loud. Finally, her sobs fade away. She is gone.)

PETE
    (Still sobbing, leaning against the door, his face hidden from the audience as he talks to them with a voice still shaking from anger and sadness.)
And that, fellow American males…
(His voice now changes from sadness to a regular tone and somewhat jubilant. He uncovers his face to show an ear-to-ear smile.)
…is how you get out of the marriage conversation!
(He laughs out loud and does a little dance around the apartment.)
Oh, she thought she had me! Did you see her? Did you see how she came at me? It was like a prize fighter on the attack.
    (He does boxing motions as he says the following exclamations.)

13

BAM! Fear of commitment! BOOM! Lusting after other women! But I took the blows. I bided my time and let her get her licks in…Then POW! I came right back at her! Turned the tables, as it were. I played the sensitivity card, threw in a few tears and heartfelt exclamations and BINGO! All of a sudden, it's all her fault! I come out as clean as a preacher's sheets! A non-Catholic preacher, of course. The way I see it, I figure I bought myself at least six more months before the next marriage and commitment talk…and, just to save the best for last, in about an hour and a half I'm going to be having the kind of sex people only see in dirty movies! In the words of Paul Simon, "Life I love you! All is groovy!"
(Fade out to Simon & Garfunkel's "The 59th Street Bridge Song")

END SCENE
CURTAIN

A Day with the Dogs

A Play in One Act

Jeremey W. Gingrich

A Day with the Dogs

A One-Act Play

Roger and Steve are friends. Good friends. The best of friends. On this day, Roger has coaxed Steve into going to the dog track. Roger is a seasoned veteran of the track, whereas Steve is a newcomer. They are both twenty-nine-years-old. Steve is married and has just opened a restaurant, while Roger is an owner of a sporting goods store and compulsive gambler. During their day at the track, Roger confesses to a provocative secret which truly calls to mind the question: "How strong are the bonds of friendship?"

Jeremey W. Gingrich

Time: The Present

Synopsis of Scenes

SCENE 1—The Ticket Counter

SCENE 2—Fred's Lounge above the Track

SCENE 3—The Track-Side Bench

SCENE 4—Fred's Lounge above the Track

SCENE 5—The Track-Side Bench

A Day with the Dogs

SCENE 1—*ROGER and STEVE are waiting in line at the ticket counter. ROGER is wearing a suit and tie, while STEVE is simply wearing a collared shirt and slacks, with a windbreaker. There are extras running around the stage, gamblers at the track, and there is also a TELLER, who takes their bet at the counter.*

ROGER

Did you tell Theresa?

STEVE

Are you kidding? I take a day off of work to come down to the dog track of all places, and spend five-hundred bucks on a dog in a wager of his speed in relation to other dogs on a frickin' circular track! No, Roger. To answer your question, no I did not tell Theresa. She'd kill me.

ROGER
(Shaking his head.)

You are so whipped.

STEVE
(Loud.)

Whipped!
(He looks around and then lowers his voice.)
Where do you get that from? Just because my wife doesn't want me throwing away five-hundred dollars and would throw a fit if she ever found out I did, and just because I would not prefer sleeping the remainder of the month on the living room sofa, does not make me whipped. I prefer the term…non-confrontational.

ROGER

Oh, please. You are in such denial! You're whipped because you are afraid to have your wife mad at you. You're scared of her yelling at you and you let her hold that power over your head. For Christ's sake, Steve, you're supposed to be the man of the house, the king of that castle.

19

STEVE

Well excuse me, tough guy! Have you ever heard my
wife yell? That woman can shatter glass when she gets
angry enough. Anyway, why are we focusing on me?
What about you, eh? Did you tell Angela?

ROGER

Are you kidding? She'd kill me.

(Pause.)

STEVE

(Becoming impatient.)

Why is this line so long anyway? It's the middle of a
workday for crying out loud!

ROGER

These people are regulars, Steve. They come here
everyday and spend hundreds of dollars on these damn
dogs. It really is a profitable industry.

STEVE

No offense, but these don't look like the type of people
who can afford that kind of excessive lifestyle. This
place is like where fashion sense goes to die. I've
never seen so much polyester and plaid. I think a
majority of these people are clothed by Goodwill.

ROGER

Well, we have to be thankful for people with this
lifestyle, Steve. My boy, Fred, he hangs out here all the
time and he's the one that gave me the tip on this dog
in the third race. He says it's a mortal lock.

STEVE

How can he be sure? Dog racing is far from an exact
science. And are you sure Fred is his real name? I
didn't think anyone had that name.

ROGER

What are you talking' about? Fred is a very common
name.

STEVE

Yeah, for a cartoon character. I don't think I've ever
met and been introduced to anyone named Fred. What

kind of parent looks at their child and says, "You know, he looks like a Fred."?

ROGER

Jeez, would you just relax. Fred knows dog racing. He wouldn't lead us wrong.

STEVE

I just can't believe I let you talk me into this. I am such a pushover.

ROGER

That's why we get along so well.

(Pause.)

Hey, we're almost to the front of the line. Get your money out.

STEVE

(Getting his wallet.)

Just tell me about the dog again.

ROGER

The name's Keep the Faith. The owners have been training him on this track for the past week and a half and the times on his practice runs have been stellar. Fred watches the practice runs, and he says Keep the Faith could easily beat any dog out here. And since he's a fairly new racer, not many people bet on him and the odds will go through the roof. We can't lose, and we'll win big.

STEVE

(Has the money out but still has not handed it to ROGER.)

Alright, but you're buying lunch. I'm starving. When is our race, anyway?

ROGER

Ours doesn't get underway until 1:00 pm.

STEVE

Good, we've got time. I saw a Chinese buffet place just across the street.

ROGER

Nah, it'd be better if we just ate in the lounge here.
Fred says it's bad luck to leave the track once you
place the bet.

STEVE

(Pulling money away.)

See, that doesn't instill a lot of confidence in me at all.
I agreed to make this bet on the conditions that it was a
logical choice…based on the facts of dog racing. Now
you bring in all this superstition nonsense and I gotta
tell ya, I'm a little uneasy. It gives me a vision of Fred
pulling this dog's name out of a hat.

ROGER

*(Motioning for the money. They are now at the
window.)*

I told you how Fred got this dog, Steve. But you have
to understand a lot of dog racing is superstition.

*(ROGER points at a man looking at dogs on the track,
holding a racing form.)*

See that guy? That's Eddie Manudo. He picks his dogs
by the lengths of their faces.

STEVE

How does that work?

ROGER

He looks at the dog's faces and bets on the one he
thinks has the longest face. He puts fifty on every odd
numbered race, and sometimes he has good days and
sometimes he goes broke, but it's all superstition.

STEVE

Well, I guess if a dog wins by a nose, it helps to have
the longer nose.

ROGER

Whatever…now can I just have the money, please.
We're holding up the line.

STEVE

Oh…okay.

(He hands the money to ROGER.)

But if Theresa ever found out I trusted you with
something like this she'd put me in an institution.

ROGER
(To STEVE, shaking his head.)
You are so whipped.
(To TELLER)
Can I have $1000 on the Number 9 to win in the third
race, please?
(The tickets are processed and handed to ROGER.)

TELLER
Nothing for the first or second? Try your luck, buddy.

ROGER
Jesus, what do you want from us? We just handed you
a grand! We're not made of money. I'll see you after
the third to collect our winnings.

STEVE
(Slaps ROGER on the arm.)
Don't jinx it, man!

ROGER
Who's superstitious now?

END SCENE 1

SCENE 2—*This takes place in a lounge on the upper deck of the
dog track. There is a counter next to the grill where STEVE and
ROGER plan to sit, but there are also tables scattered about. There is
an overlook where they can see the track. There is a door on the side
of the lounge opposite from the counter for the men's room. There is a
woman sitting at the counter, having a drink. There is a cook at the
grill, flipping burgers. This is FRED, a large, black man with an
apron spattered with grease. There is a waitress running around the
tables, taking orders.*

STEVE
What kind of stuff they serve here?

ROGER

Anything from the grilled and fried food groups. I
recommend the hamburgers and onion rings. Oh, and
their corn dogs are really something else!

STEVE

Corn dogs? No thanks.

ROGER

Why not?

STEVE

C'mon, Rog, you know what's in a hot dog. Even
thinking about it makes me nauseous.

ROGER

Yeah, but a corn dog uses a protective fried outer
covering to hide the fact that you're eating a hot dog.
Just try these dogs, Steve, you'll love 'em.

STEVE

Y'know, just one day in my life I would like to display
a little backbone and not let you talk me into
everything.

ROGER

But until that day…

*(ROGER motions his hand towards a stool at the
counter. STEVE sits down and ROGER quickly
follows. The waitress comes out to take their orders.
The cook, FRED, still has his back to them, working
the grill.)*

ROGER

(To the waitress)

Two burgers and two corn dogs, please. Oh, and what
did you want to drink, Steve?

STEVE

Coke, no ice.

ROGER

(Looks at STEVE for a second.)

Okay, and could we have two Pepsi's, please. One
with no ice.

(Pause, as the waitress leaves to put in the order.)

24

What is it with you and the no ice, anyway, eh Steve? The refills here are free. It doesn't matter if the ice takes up space, because you can always fill that space back up. That's what a refill is, you know?

STEVE

Roger, we've discussed this before.

ROGER

Well, just refresh my memory.

(The waitress hands them their drinks.)

STEVE

I dislike ice because it forces me to drink faster than my desired pace. Because, if I don't drink fast, the ice melts in the drink and waters it down, eventually leaving me with a disgusting glass of brown water. Besides, when drinking from a glass with ice, said ice obstructs the free flow of soda from the glass to my lips.

(He uses his glass as an example.)

Ice is like underwear, Roger. I don't need it, and it only gets in the way.

(After this last line, a woman sitting next to STEVE moves two seats away from him. There is a pause as STEVE and ROGER watch her move.)

ROGER

You know what I think?

STEVE

I have a feeling you're going to tell me.

ROGER

I just think it's your way of standing out…Making a point.

STEVE

And what point is that?

ROGER

You're trying to announce to everyone who hears you that…

(Mocking voice.)

"Hey, look at me everybody. I am a different person. I get no ice in my drink, so I'm special." It's your little way of getting attention.

STEVE

Please, Roger, you know I hate attention. I don't deal well with people.

ROGER

Maybe this is your way of overcoming that.

STEVE

Oh, I'm sorry, Roger. Maybe I'm mistaken but the last time I checked, you worked at a sporting goods store. So you'll have to excuse me if I don't accept your psychological analysis.

(The cook turns around to hand the two their burgers and corn dogs.)

ROGER

Analysis my a…

(ROGER recognizes the cook. It's FRED.)

Hey, Fred! I didn't even see you there, man. How you doin'?

(They shake hands.)

FRED

Hey, Rog.

STEVE

Fred?

ROGER

Oh, I'm sorry, I'm such an idiot. Steven Edwards, this is Fred Williamson. This man knows these races like nobody else.

(STEVE shakes hands with FRED but his face has a look of surprise on it that hasn't left his face since ROGER said FRED's name. FRED smiles.)

FRED

Steve, right? Yeah, I remember you talkin' about your buddy Steve, Rog.

(Back to STEVE.)

26

You know, man, you let that wife of yours walk all over you. Theresa, is that it?

(STEVE nods slowly with the same expression of surprise on his face.)

I would just say to her, whenever she got in one of her uppity moods, "Listen up, Theresa! I am the man of this house and you will not be yellin' up in here all the time…"

STEVE

(Interrupting)

Yeah thanks, Fred. Do you mind if I have a word with Roger for a minute? Thanks.

(STEVE pulls ROGER to the back of the lounge to the spot that overlooks the track., out of earshot of FRED.)

ROGER

What? What is it?

STEVE

(Losing control.)

What is it? I'll tell you what it is! It's Fred, damn it! I can't believe you! I will never trust you with anything again!

ROGER

What? What about Fred? Oh, okay, maybe I shouldn't have blabbed about my particular views on your marriage. I'll concede that it's probably strange to hear a total stranger talk about your life. But if you'd just listen to his suggestions…

STEVE

(Still frantic.)

Not that! I don't care about that! I care about the fact that I put five hundred dollars on the investment advice of a fry cook! A fry cook, Roger!

ROGER

Well, what did you think he did, I told you he worked at the track.

STEVE

I thought he was a trainer or maybe an owner or
something!

ROGER

(Still dismissive of his frantic mood.)
Oh, Fred couldn't afford to be an owner. He's only a
fry cook, for God's sake. Owning a racing dog costs…

STEVE

This is not the point! Jesus Christ! Theresa will never
let me forget this, man. I could have used that money
at the restaurant! You know every dime counts with a
new business!

ROGER

(Now getting upset himself.)
I am sick and tired of hearing about you and your
restaurant, Steve! I know it was a risk you took by
starting a business, and I know it is a pain in the ass,
but for Christ's sake you have got to stop whining
about it all the time! People start businesses as an
adventurous undertaking, which is meant to bring
some joy into their lives. You make it sound like it
wasn't worth it! But no, Steve, if you're so worried
about this race, let's just test Fred's knowledge of the
track, eh?

STEVE

(Argument and anger dying down.)
But if Theresa…

ROGER

For crying out loud, Steve, if I hear you say her name
one more time I will throw you out of this fricking
window.
(ROGER now looks out the window down at the track.)
Look. The first race is about to start.

STEVE

(Calm and a bit embarrassed.)
So?

ROGER
(Walks over to FRED at the counter.)
Hey, Fred. Who you like in the first?
(FRED is hesitant. ROGER coaxes him.)
C'mon, it's Roger!

FRED
(He succumbs and looks around then leans in to whisper to ROGER, though it's still audible to STEVE across the room.)
The number 2 is the favorite, but I think the 7 dog will take it by at least two lengths.

STEVE
(His interest peaked.)
How can you be so sure?

FRED
I pass by the dogs every morning before I start work. When I passed by 7's pen…he just looked like he wanted it more.

STEVE
(Flabbergasted. Stuttering.)
The dog…The dog looked like he wanted it more?

FRED
(A bit insulted.)
Yeah. He had a look about him that said he really wants to win this race.

STEVE
(Still looking straight at FRED. Talking slowly.)
Well…that's…great, Fred. Thanks. Thanks for that.

ROGER
(Sensing his skepticism, because it's pretty blatant.)
Look, Steve, if Fred says it's the number 7 that is who will win. I told you, nobody…

STEVE
(Interrupting. Loud and angry.)
Yeah, yeah. "Nobody knows these dogs like your boy, Fred."
(He walks away.)

ROGER

Where are you going? The race is about to begin, and
we got food here.

STEVE

I'm going to the bathroom. You and Dr. Doolittle stay
put…I might be a while.
*(He pauses and turns around when he reaches the
bathroom door.)*
I have to figure out how to explain to Theres…
*(He doesn't complete the name, and he eyeballs
ROGER.)*
…to my wife how I lost five hundred dollars of the
restaurant's petty cash.
*(He kicks the bathroom door open and exits into the
Men's Room.)*

ROGER
(Yelling at the door.)
Just be sure to get out here for the race!
(Walks over to FRED at the counter.)
Can you believe that guy?

FRED
(Now back at the grill, flipping burgers.)
Why do you hang out with him anyway? You two are
complete opposites. Most friends have stuff in
common, but your personalities are entirely different.

ROGER

When he's not bitching about his restaurant, or his
wife, or any of his other numerous problems, he's a
decent guy to be around.

FRED

But with the way you go on about him all the time, I'd
have thought of him as your best friend. When you're
best friends with someone, they have to be more than
just "a decent guy to be around."

ROGER

That's not all there is to him, Fred. You're only seeing
one side of him today.

30

(Pause.)
Steve's a…Steve's like a favorite song. What's your favorite song, Fred? Favorite song of all time.

FRED
(Thinks for a bit.)
"Ain't no woman…" No. "Just my imagination" by the Temptations. Why?

ROGER
Why that song? What makes that song better than all other songs? What do you love about it?

FRED
(Flummoxed.)
Well…It's a lot of little things altogether, really.
(Scraping at the grill.)
There's the lead vocals, followed by the harmony of the backup singers. The intro is fantastic and the lyrics always…
(He looks around. Then leans in to ROGER, whispering.)
The lyrics sometimes get to me. I sometimes…Sometimes I start to well up…I almost cry.

ROGER
(Loud.)
You cry from the Temptations?!

FRED
(Defensively loud, looking around.)
No! I did not cry! I said I felt like crying. I didn't cry from no song! Anyway, I thought we were talking about Steve here. What's he got to do with the Temptations?

ROGER
Well, when you're best friends with someone like Steve, explaining that relationship is like explaining why you like your favorite song. There are different and numerous reasons why you like it, but in the end you still don't know the full reason.

31

FRED

But surely there must be one reason that sticks out in your head.

ROGER

Well…there is one. You see, Steve was going out with my wife, Angie, before I ever met her. He introduced us, and eventually, when things fell through with them, she started going out with me and we eventually got married.

FRED

Wow.

ROGER

Yeah, but that's not the best part. Steve eventually met Theresa and married her so everything was fine, you know…nobody felt left out. But two years into my marriage, Angela was getting scared. She thought she might've made a mistake getting married at 23 and all. She even thought I wasn't mature enough to handle marriage. Can you believe that?

FRED

Women.

ROGER

That's what I said. But there was nothing I could say to change her mind, and for three weeks she went and stayed at her mother's. I could've lost my wife, man.

FRED

What happened?

ROGER

Well, eventually Steve went over to Angie and talked with her on my behalf, since she wouldn't let me anywhere near the house. And after this meeting, the next day in fact, Angie moved back in with me, apologized for freaking out, and we've been happily married ever since.

FRED

That's great, Rog. What did Steve say to her to change her mind?

ROGER

Well, I haven't managed to get the whole conversation out of him, but he did tell me one thing he said, and that line sticks in my head whenever I think of Steven.

(FRED leans in and ROGER makes sure he hears the line, saying it slowly and clearly.)

He said to Angie, "Marriage is scary. Hell, life is scary, Angela. But you and I are lucky." He told her, "We're lucky because we chose someone as great as Roger to help us through the scary times. He loves you and you two should be together."

(After this line, ROGER leans back on his stool, content at the point he's made. FRED stands up straight.)

FRED

(After a pause, blubbering.)

That's…that's beautiful, man.

(STEVE comes out of the bathroom.)

STEVE

Okay, Rog. Here's what happened. I took out the petty cash to buy some more silverware…When all of a sudden we got jumped by three guys on the street and they took my money clip with the five hund…

(In mid-sentence, FRED grabs STEVE from behind the counter and gives him a big hug, still blubbering.)

FRED

That's beautiful, man.

STEVE

(Standing still, letting himself be hugged by this large black man.)

Did I miss something?

(FRED pulls away and quickly turns back to the grill, concealing his face.)

STEVE

(Listens to FRED sob for a while.)

Are you…are you crying, Fred?

FRED
(Sobbing.)
No! I…I just got through cutting some onions, that's all.
(He turns to quickly exit to the kitchen.)
I better get some more from the back.
(FRED exits to get more onions and to cry in solitude.)
STEVE
What was that all about?
ROGER
Fred's just a real emotional guy, Steve. He'll be fine.
STEVE
Okay, then, did you hear the plan? We were jumped by three guys, you got it? We tried to fight them off, but…
(The horn for the first race interrupts Steve's thought.)
ROGER
Shut up, Steve.
(ROGER gets off the stool and goes behind the counter to yell at FRED in the kitchen.)
Get out here, Fred. The first race is starting.
(ROGER and STEVE walk over to the window to watch the race, FRED stumbles out with arms full of onions.)
ROGER
Here we go.
(The Loudspeaker announces "They're off." ROGER gets immediately excited, he points down to the race.)
Look at that, Steve! Right out of the gate, 7's in the lead!
STEVE
(Anxious and worried.)
There's still a lot of track to go, Roger.
ROGER
Come on, 7! Keep that lead!
FRED
Whoa! The 2 dog is coming up quick.

ROGER

Come on, 7! Come on, 7!

STEVE

(Now just very excited.)

The 2 is falling back!

FRED

7 is in the lead by more than 3 lengths!

ROGER

Go ahead, 7! Alright, baby!

(The Loudspeaker announces "And the winner of the first race...Number 7!" As this is announced, FRED, STEVE, and ROGER all jump, scream and celebrate like little boys. Onions fly everywhere.)

ROGER

What did I tell you, Steve?

STEVE

(Laughing.)

I know, Rog. I know. "Nobody knows these races like your boy, Fred!"

(They all exchange high-fives.)

FRED

(After much laughter and celebration, FRED notices his onions strewn about the floor.)

Oh, damn. My onions.

(He crawls around to pick up the surrounding onions. STEVE and ROGER laugh at FRED picking up the onions, then progress from a high-five, to a hand shake, to a hug.)

END SCENE 2

SCENE 3—*ROGER and STEVE are sitting beside the track now, in a gallery where there are about ten big-screen TV's simulcasting the tracks around the country. They are at a small table to one side of the stage, and on the other side of the stage, there is a bench that* *overlooks the track, next to a pillar. STEVE is writing on a racing form while ROGER is watching one of the screens.*

STEVE

What are you watching?

ROGER

There's a race up in Jersey going on right now. I think the Number 4 is gonna take it, but I wouldn't bet the farm, if you know what I mean.

STEVE

(Looking up and surveying all the screens.)
You mean all these TV's are broadcasting different races from around the country?

ROGER

Yeah, Steve. They call it simulcasting. You remember those big satellites we saw when we drove in?

STEVE

Yeah.

ROGER

All of those transmit broadcasts of other races throughout the circuit, and the feeds are directly simultaneous with the time of the race, hence the name "simulcast."
(He points to the different screens.)
That one's Jersey. That one's Philadelphia. Over there is Miami, and those other one's transmit from the tracks in the South.

STEVE

And you can place bets from here on all those different tracks in all those different cities?

ROGER

(Still watching his Jersey race.)
Damn it, the 4 came in third. I think that first dog pushed him.
(Now back to STEVE.)
Oh yeah, on any given day you can place bets on hundreds of different races, even though this track only runs twelve a day.

STEVE

Boy, they sure do open every avenue for the shills to hand over their money. You know the problem is most of these guys are addicted. These track owners are like dealers, feeding a habit. It's really quite heartless.

ROGER

They're no different from the rest of us, Steve-O.

STEVE

What do you mean, "the rest of us?"

ROGER

Think about it. We're all in the business of making money. I sell basketballs, you sell French fries, these guys sell…

STEVE

Sell what? They don't sell anything, Roger. These people, these track owners and ticket sellers, they feed on the stupidity and weakness of the masses. They sell pieces of paper to hundreds of people trying to make a quick buck, instead of earning it through blood, sweat and tears.

ROGER

Are they the guys that sang "Dancing in September?" Or was that Earth, Wind and Fire? I always get those two mixed up. Anyway, as for the people trying to make a quick buck, isn't that exactly what you're trying to do?

STEVE

Don't you dare group me in the same category as these track rats! I'm here based on the investment advice of a friend.

ROGER

Yeah, a friend who told you he had a quick way to make some cash. Don't try to act so high and mighty around these people, Steve. You're in the same boat with all of them. We're all here trying to stretch our money a little further, and at great risk I might add. And as far as the owners go, they're only trying to make money providing a service, just like us. So, despite what you might think, you are no better than anyone at this track.

STEVE

(Humbled but dismissive of ROGER's point.)

Anyway, I'm still gonna enjoy taking this place's money.

ROGER

We both will. What have you been working on anyway?

STEVE

(Pointing down to the racing form he has been writing on.)

Oh, this? I've just been working out what to do with the winnings.

ROGER

(Apprehensive.)

The winnings?

STEVE

Yeah. From what I can tell, it works out great. This form has Keep the Faith running at 10 to 1, and if those odds hold, I'll have five thousand dollars to spend at the restaurant. I've had my eyes on this antique jukebox I saw on the Internet last month. I think it would look great in that area next to the kitchen. I might even have enough left over to buy Theresa something nice. What do you think?

ROGER

Steve, you're going about this all wrong.

STEVE

What do you mean?

ROGER

When you bet on a race, you have to think that the money you put down is gone, that you've thrown it away. You can never think of the money you might win. No good can come from that.

38

STEVE

What are you talking about?

ROGER

If you start to think about all the things you'll buy once
you win: the antique jukebox, some jewelry for
Theresa, a gift for me…

STEVE

I didn't say anything about a gift for you.

ROGER

(Shoots him a quick mean glance.)

Yeah, I know. Anyway, if you start to think about
buying all those things, you'll think you've lost all
those things if you lose. You must remember at all
times that you put five hundred dollars down to
purchase these little pieces of paper…

(He holds up the win tickets.)

…and that is all. You see, with all your calculations
and planned purchases, if by some chance we lose…by
some slim chance…you'll beat yourself up thinking
that you lost five thousand dollars worth of cash and
prizes, when in reality, you never had five thousand
dollars in the first place. You always have to think
small, Steve…or not at all. That's the method that
works best for me.

STEVE

Where do you come up with this stuff?

ROGER

I was raised at places like this, buddy. My father taught
me everything he knew. The man was a wizard at the
track.

STEVE

I remember you saying something about your father's
gambling problem. He took you to the track…as a kid?

ROGER

Oh yeah. All the time. You don't pick up this kind of
knowledge overnight. My dad taught me how to read a
Racing Form before he taught me about the birds and

the bees, a conversation we also had at the track. He taught me about the simulcasts, how the odds come out, all the different bets you can make on a race: the exacta, the trifecta, win, place, show…all that stuff. And it wasn't just dogs, either.

STEVE

Horses, too?

ROGER

Yeah, dad loved the horse races. Especially the Triple Crown. But he also had a real affinity for chariot races.

STEVE

Chariot races?

ROGER

Yeah, it's just like a horse race, except the jockeys ride behind the horses on two-wheeled chariots. It's a little different, but the premise stays the same.

STEVE

(Laughing at the concept.)

Do the jockeys where gladiator armor or shit like that?

ROGER

No, it's not "Ben-Hur," smart-ass. It's just guys riding around a track in a cart pulled by a horse, inspired by a whip. It's considered a sport.

STEVE

And the animal rights people are okay with this?

ROGER

Everything's on the up and up. The only problem people really have with the whole horse racing system, chariot or no chariot, is that, you know, if a horse breaks a leg or comes up lame after a race…the owners opt to destroy him. You know, bullet to the temple…goodnight.

STEVE

Yeah, I remember hearing that about race horses. Jeez, talk about pressure.

ROGER

What?

STEVE

Think about it. Put yourself in the horse's shoes.
(He chuckles at his little unintended pun.)
You're well fed, daily bathed, having a good life in a
cool, comfortable stable, but every time you
race...every time you participate in this sport...you
face the realization that if you injure yourself, you're
gonna get killed. Imagine if NBA players had to face
that consequence. The sports page's injury report
would be synonymous with the obituaries. I mean, if I
woke up to that type of reality every morning, I'd be
paranoid at every crack in the road.

ROGER

You're serious.

STEVE

Yeah. It has to be very stressful.

ROGER

Steven, you're talking about the mentality of a horse.
An animal, for crying out loud. He doesn't get
paranoid or worry about getting shot. All he does is
eat, sleep and run, and that's all he knows! I can't
believe we had a serious conversation about the mental
stability and job security of a horse.

STEVE

*(Embarrassed, quickly changing the subject, pointing
towards the track.)*
Look, they're bringing the dogs out for the next race.
Let's get better seats.
*(They move to a spot closer to the track next to the
pillar.)*

ROGER

Alright, Steve, who do you like out of these guys?
Let's test your knowledge. What have we learned so
far?

STEVE

Well, I'm no Fred, but I think the 6 dog looks good.

41

ROGER
(He's eyeing all the dogs.)
Looks like a good dog. No, no, it's gotta be the 1.
STEVE
Why Number 1?

ROGER
Look at him. He's taking a shit right now, right on the track.

STEVE
(Making an unpleasant face.)
And that's relevant because…

ROGER
Think about it, Steve, he just got rid of some excess baggage. He'll be that much lighter on his feet and therefore faster in the race. I'm positive about this one. It's a lock.

STEVE
That's the worst logic I've ever heard. After you use the bathroom, you're so relaxed you don't even want to move, let alone run an entire race. Now, you find me a dog that has to shit real bad, and that dog is the winner. I know I run hella fast when I'm running to the bathroom when it's crunch time.

ROGER
Disgusting as it may be…you've got a point there.
(They both slightly laugh, enjoying the levity of the conversation, watching the dogs getting ready for the race. STEVE lets his attention be pulled away by a nice looking girl passing by him in a midriff shirt with a tattoo of a dolphin on the small of her back. He chuckles out loud.)
ROGER
What's funny?

STEVE
Nothing. It's just…that girl's tattoo. I find it…amusing, that's all. The dolphin and what not.

ROGER
*(Looking in the general direction of the fine girl,
chuckling along with STEVE.)*
Oh yeah. It's just like Theresa's only a little bigger.
*(As ROGER says this, his eyes grow wide, wide with
the knowledge that he has let something slip. After he
says this, the Loudspeaker starts the second race by
announcing, "And they're off!")*
STEVE
(Stuttering. Taken off guard.)
What…What do you mean…"just like Theresa's?"
How do you know…What do you mean?
ROGER
(Searching in his head for the right answer.)
You know, Theresa's tattoo. The dolphin…it's like the
girl's.
(Changing the subject.)
Wow, you're Number 6 is looking good.
STEVE
Roger, Theresa's tattoo was a special gift for me, her
husband. It's on her upper and inner left thigh.
(He is gravely serious.)
How do you know about her tattoo?
ROGER
(Still searching his brain for the right answer.)
She…she told me about it one time. We were…we
were discussing tattoos and stuff like that and she…she
told me she had a dolphin tattoo such as that.
STEVE
*(Very serious and deliberately staring at ROGER, who
is trying to avoid his gaze.)*
Roger, we haven't told anyone about the tattoo. It was
meant as a family secret just between us. She doesn't
like people knowing about it. So I must ask again, how
do you know about my wife's tattoo?
ROGER
(Panicking.)

43

You know, you're missing a great race here.
STEVE
(Very loud and angry.)
Forget the damn race, Roger! How do you know about
Theresa's upper thigh?
ROGER
(He gets up from the bench to pace as he thinks.)
Okay, okay. Theresa…Theresa was out in a bathing
suit one time, getting some sun or something…and I
was…I was checking her out, okay? You caught me,
I'm sorry. I was checking out your wife. I'm not proud
of it…I feel real guilty, but…
STEVE
*(Calm and deliberate at first, but gradually losing
control of his rage.)*
Well, that would be a touching apology, Roger, except
for the fact that my wife doesn't even own a bathing
suit, because she freckles in the sun, and has never
swam a day in her life!
*(STEVE gets up from the bench and runs over to
ROGER, grabbing him by the lapels and thrusting him
against the pillar next to the bench. This is why we
need a pillar.)*
Now, I'm gonna ask you one more time, Roger. How
do you know about my wife's tattoo?
ROGER
*(Totally at the mercy of STEVE's rage, still pinned up
against the pillar. He succumbs to the inquisition and
lets slip the story.)*
Alright, alright! I'll tell you the truth! About two
months ago, I went over to your house to ask you to a
baseball game. I had just gotten tickets from a friend of
mine to a doubleheader and I wanted to see if you
could go. But when I went in, you weren't home. It
was the middle of the day, and you were apparently
doing something at the restaurant…But
Theresa…Theresa was there.

*(STEVE's grip loosens and he slowly slinks back down
to the bench, as he realizes where the story is going.)*
We talked for a while, had some wine…She said she
felt alone…I was trying to comfort her…She said you
were spending all your time at the restaurant and she
was lonely…I only tried to make her feel better. Next
thing I knew…we were naked on the couch together.
I'm really sorry, Steve, I never meant for it to
happen…It was an accident, I swear, and that was the
only time, I promise.

STEVE
(In shock, sitting on the bench.)
That's my favorite couch. I watch TV on that couch.

ROGER
Steve? Steve, are you okay?

STEVE
I feel…I feel nauseous. I feel physically sick…
(His anger builds up.)
Now…Now I feel physically angry.

ROGER
(Backing away as STEVE clenches his fists.)
What…What does that mean?

STEVE
*(In an angry rage, STEVE springs from the bench and
lunges at ROGER's neck, choking him against the
pillar.)*
I'm gonna ring your fucking neck, you back-stabbing
son of a bitch! I can't believe you did this to me! This
is my wife, damn it! This is my family!

ROGER
(In a gurgled panic.)
Steve, what are you doing?

STEVE
*(STEVE's strength is dwindling and his anger is
turning into sobbing emotion. He sinks back to the
bench with his head in his hands.)*
This is my family. This is my life.

ROGER
(Loosening his collar.)
I'm telling you, Steven, it was a one time thing and
purely accidental.

STEVE
(Emotion-filled yelling.)
Don't say that! Don't dismiss it like that. This was not
an accident. This is a continual representation of your
ongoing effort to destroy everything I've ever owned
or loved!

ROGER
What?

STEVE
Am I supposed to believe this is just a mix up? Some
unfortunate incident of happenstance? A bad day at the
old Edwards household? Jesus, Roger, you slept with
my wife, for God's sake! It's not like you dented my
car…

ROGER
(Ashamed, looking at his hands.)
Ooh, you saw that?

STEVE
(Added shock.)
You dented my car?

ROGER
A little bit, on the passenger side, you can barely
notice it…from far away. I thought you knew?

STEVE
My God, Roger, I was just making an analogy for
effect. Is there anything else I should know? What, did
you kick my dog or something?

ROGER
Come on, you know I'd never do that. I love Scruffy.
*(At this comment, STEVE just looks at ROGER for a
pause, then collects his things from the bench and
starts to walk off.)*
Where are you going?

STEVE

Away from you.

ROGER

What does that mean?

STEVE

(Has walked to the edge of the stage and turned to face him.)

Are you that stupid? It means I am severing all bonds with you, Roger. It means, as far as I'm concerned, Roger Walton doesn't exist anymore. The only possible time your name will ever come up will be at my divorce proceedings.

ROGER

Divorce proceedings? Steven, you're overreacting.

STEVE

(Turns to face ROGER, a look of disbelief on his face.)

Overreacting? I'm overreacting? My best friend sleeps with my wife, I haven't shot anyone, and I'm overreacting? What am I supposed to do? Sit around with a Coke and a smile while the whole thing goes on?

ROGER

It's not going on, Steven. It was a one time thing, I swear! It went on once, and she's been faithful to you ever since.

(STEVE blows him off and walks away. ROGER yells after him as he exits the stage.)

And besides, I think your overlooking your blame in all this!

STEVE

(Storming back on the stage.)

I gotta hear this.

(He throws his jacket and papers back on the bench.)

Okay, Roger, what is my part in all this? Enlighten me. Did I put some big sign over my wife that said, "Sleep with me!" or something.

ROGER

No, you sarcastic bastard, but you were behind the wheel when she was driven to another man.

STEVE

And how did I do that, oh master of analogies?

ROGER

You had been working on that restaurant non-stop for four months before the affair occurred. We're talking late nights and early mornings, pal. Theresa was lonely. Four months is a long time to be alone, Steve. Theresa is a woman who needs love and affection, and for a long time you weren't there to give it to her. If she didn't get it from me, she would've gotten it from somewhere else.

STEVE

Oh! So I guess I should thank you, is that it? It's so good to know that in my absence, my good friend Roger could step up to the plate and keep my wife warm for me. Thanks, Rog! At least it wasn't the milkman or the FedEx guy, right?

ROGER

For a whole year you have done nothing but eat, sleep and dream that restaurant. It has been your obsession, an unhealthy one at that, and your wife has supported you throughout the whole thing. Hell, so have I. But throughout the whole year, you have overlooked both of us in the pursuit of your final goal. Maybe the occasional "thank you" or kiss on the cheek could have prevented the whole thing, but we'll never know because you never tried those, did you? All that mattered was the restaurant. Well, congratulations, Steve! You've got your damn restaurant! Are you happy?

STEVE

Are you finished?

(ROGER folds his arms, content with the point he just made.)

48

STEVE
(In a low, slow, deliberate voice.)
Theresa and I were joined under the bonds of love and the eyes of God to be together for the rest of our lives, and none of your smoke and mirrors will be able to disguise the fact that you took that from us, Roger.
(STEVE turns away, grabs his things, and walks offstage.)
ROGER
(Calling after STEVE who is offstage.)
Steven…Steve you can't leave me! You're the best friend I've got, man!
(Now low and to himself.)
You're the best friend I've got.

END SCENE 3

SCENE 4—*Back up in the lounge. STEVE is drinking another Coke with no ice, while FRED is tending to the grill. A woman, DIXIE, walks in and sits one stool away from STEVE. She is a classy, beautiful working girl in a tight miniskirt. STEVE just sits there sulking and drinking for quite a while.*
STEVE
Hey, Fred. I don't suppose you sell anything a little stronger than the buzz I get from a Pepsi, do you?
FRED
Well, I sell Michelob and Budweiser back here, too. But something about you demands more, am I right?
STEVE
Your insight is staggering. And besides, I can't stand the taste of beer.
FRED
(He looks around, suspicious of his customers. Then jokes with STEVE.)

By the tone of your voice and the manner of your
actions, I can see you need a physician, my boy.
Paging Dr. Daniels. Dr. Jack Daniels.
*(He pulls a bottle of Jack Daniels from behind the
counter and pours it into STEVE's cup.)*

STEVE

You're a good man, Fred.

FRED

One of the best, my man. One of the best.
*(DIXIE moves one seat closer to STEVE and starts
talking to him.)*

DIXIE

(Leaning in confidently to STEVE.)
A man only turns to the doctor when he has real
problems.

STEVE

Your insight is staggering.

DIXIE

You already said that.

STEVE

Oh…sorry. I'm Steve…resident loser. Nice to meet
you.

DIXIE

I'm Dixie.
(She eyeballs him for a while.)
You've got women problems, don't you?

STEVE

(Looking up from his cup.)
It shows, don't it?

DIXIE

Well, I've been the cause of those looks for many
different guys. The guys may change, but the looks
stay the same. You want to talk about it?

STEVE

Not especially, no.

DIXIE

It'll make you feel better.

STEVE

It'll make me feel better? Why does everybody say that? How can discussing a problem possibly make anyone feel better? If you ignore a problem long enough, it goes away, and yet everyone seems to think that the easiest way to alleviate yourself of your problems is to bring them up over and over again. Just once I would like to not discuss a problem. Just this once I would like to leave it alone.

DIXIE

Fine with me, pal. Just trying to help, that's all.
(She moves back to her original stool.)

STEVE

(After a long pause, STEVE looks at his glass for a while and then eventually moves to the stool beside DIXIE.)
I just...I just found out that my wife of seven years cheated on me.

DIXIE

Ouch.

STEVE

You're damn right, "Ouch." And as icing on the cake, she slept with my best friend, too. How's that for a kick in the teeth?

DIXIE

Wow! How long has it been going on?

STEVE

Well, it wasn't actually "going on" because he said it only happened once. He's trying to play it off as a crime of passion or something.

DIXIE

Well, do you believe him? I mean, the guy slept with your wife, for crying out loud. It's not inconceivable that he could lie about how often he has done it.

STEVE

No, it was just the one time. You see, with Roger, I can always tell when he's lying to my face. He tries it every once in a while, but I can spot it. He has a look about him…almost like he's scared…like a deer caught in headlights.

(He chuckles to himself.)

DIXIE

Sounds like you two were close.

STEVE

Since we were kids. Hell, I introduced him to his wife. We went to college together and we've stuck together to help each other on both our businesses.

DIXIE

What business are you two in?

STEVE

He owns a sporting goods store and I run a restaurant.

DIXIE

Really? What kind of restaurant?

STEVE

It's one of those 1950's nostalgia café's, you know, playing old songs over the speakers, a bunch of 50's pictures and memorabilia on the walls. Roger said I only opened that type of restaurant to try and explain why my wardrobe comes straight out of "Leave it to Beaver."

(He looks down with nostalgia, and chuckles.)

Yeah, Roger and I have been through a lot together.

DIXIE

Are you prepared to throw all that away over a moment of weakness?

STEVE

(He gets upset.)

Moment of weakne…Jeez, I knew you'd take his side! I am the victim here, you know!

DIXIE

Hey, hey. Calm down. I wouldn't take this Roger guy's side. He's an obvious scumbag. I wouldn't give him the time of day. But it sounds like your feelings toward him are a little conflicted, am I right?

STEVE
(In denial of the conflict.)
No. He's a piece of...he's a piece of work, I'll tell you
that. Just when I think he doesn't care about anything
but himself, he'll surprise me. He's full of surprises.

DIXIE
You think maybe a guy like that deserves another
chance?

STEVE
(Still in denial of his feelings.)
No! No, he doesn't. He really doesn't! He does not
deserve another chance. He does not.

DIXIE
But...

STEVE
*(He finishes his drink with one big gulp and gets up
from his stool, putting some cash on the counter for his
drink.)*
But...But I'll give him one. Hey, Fred. You know
where Roger might be?

FRED
Well, the third race is coming up, and that's the one
ya'll put money on...So, I'd guess he'd want a track-
side seat.

STEVE
(To FRED.)
Thanks.
(He turns to DIXIE.)
Thank you, ma'am.

DIXIE
Really, it was nothing.
*(STEVE exits. After he is gone, ROGER steps out onto
the stage, though he has not been seen the whole time,
he had been watching and listening to the whole
exchange.)*

ROGER
(He hands DIXIE a $20 dollar bill, and speaks to her in a condescending, sarcastic tone.)
Yeah, "Thank you, ma'am." Although I thought the "obvious scumbag" comment was a little unnecessary.

DIXIE
(Putting the $20 dollar bill in her bra.)
Hey, Rog, I call them like I see them. Besides, that guy there is too good for the likes of you.

ROGER
(Defensive.)
I'll thank you not to place judgement on "the likes of me," Dixie. Fred…
(Pointing at the bottle of JD.)
…you think I can get a shot of that?

FRED
Coming right up.
(FRED gets out a shot glass and pours a shot of JD.)

DIXIE
What are you going to say to him? You can't lie your way out of this, so I'm pretty sure you're out of your area of expertise.

ROGER
You heard him.
(ROGER downs the shot and gives a thankful nod to FRED.)
He said he was going to give me another chance. All the work has been done. All I have to do is…not screw it up.

DIXIE
Also not your area of expertise.

ROGER
Hey, what is it with you, anyway? You've been busting my balls ever since Steve was in here.

DIXIE
I'm sorry, Roger. It's just that he seemed like such a nice guy. The man has a genuine affection for you. I

just…I just can't help but think of what an asshole you must be to sleep with his wife.

ROGER

Hey, hey, hey, easy on the "asshole" remarks, alright? I know I'm not going to win any Humanitarian Awards. I know I'm a son of a bitch. All I want is my best friend back. You were just a tool I used to achieve that. You did your job and I thank you. I don't really see how your opinion is really relevant here.

DIXIE

(Attitude is showing up.)

What am I? The mindless hired hand here? Screw you, Roger! You forget, my friend, I could blow this whole reconciliation for you if that poor schmuck out there found out I was a tool of yours. Did you think of that?

ROGER

Where is all this animosity coming from, Dixie? You know me. This incident with Steve's wife was a one time thing. It's not like I make infidelity a habit or anything.

DIXIE

You might want to retract that statement, Roger.

ROGER

Retract that statement? What, are we on "Law & Order" here?

FRED

(Doing his best impression of a judge.)

Does the defendant wish to retract the previous statement?

ROGER

(ROGER and DIXIE take on the roles of lawyers.)

No, your honor, I do not wish to retract said statement. I request that opposing council bring up one instance, other than the aforementioned occasion, in which I have exhibited any tendency towards infidelity…Oh.

(He recalls an occasion.)

55

DIXIE

Aha! Your honor, I stipulate that the defendant has recalled a certain instance, about eight months ago, if I remember correctly, in which such a tendency was displayed. A day in which he had particularly good fortune at this very track. A day in which he won…what? 700 dollars?

ROGER

Seven hundred and eighty.

DIXIE

And on this day, the defendant, whose wife happened to be out of town, needed someone with whom to "celebrate" this wonderful occasion.

FRED

(Banging a salt shaker like a gavel.)

Does the defendant wish to rebut this heinous…

ROGER

(Interrupting.)

Shut-up, Fred. It just got real.

(ROGER takes a pause, looking at his hands. Now back to DIXIE.)

That…that wasn't a particularly proud moment in my life, Dixie.

DIXIE

It wasn't exactly a red letter day on my calendar, either. Look, I don't bring this up to hold it against you, alright. I'm not going to tell your wife or this Steve guy. It's not exactly good for business. I just…Hell, I don't know.

FRED

(Slowly.)

Hey, Rog. The third race is about to start…and you've still gotta find Steve.

ROGER

Yeah, I know. Well, I gotta…I gotta go now.

(Turns to leave, then turns back to DIXIE.)

Wish me luck?

DIXIE
(After a reluctant pause.)
Yeah…I guess…Good luck, Roger.
*(ROGER leaves. As he does, FREDC pours two more
shots of Jack Daniels, and FRED and DIXIE down the
shots.)*
FRED and DIXIE
You're gonna need it.

END SCENE 4

SCENE 5—*ROGER walks up to see STEVE sitting on a track-side
bench, looking at a Racing Form. There is a random on-looker
watching the track that only has one line, so he can come out later.
We'll call him JOE. The bench faces out towards the audience, and
there is a rail to the front of the stage that represents the side of the
track, where the action is.*
ROGER
*(He speaks calmly and slowly, as he doesn't want to
push his luck.)*
Steve? Buddy? Have you…Have you calmed down a
bit?
STEVE
(Not looking up from the form.)
Sit down, Roger.
*(ROGER sits down next to STEVE on the bench. There
is a long pause, and STEVE does not even look up
from his Racing Form.)*
ROGER
Steve?

STEVE
(Finally lowering his form.)
You remember the time Theresa got into that big car
wreck about three years ago?
ROGER
How could I forget that? You were hysterical.

                              STEVE
I remember…I remember you stayed at the hospital
with me for two nights straight and even closed the
store on a Saturday to make sure she was alright, and
to keep me calm.
                              ROGER
Well, you would've done the same for me. It was…It
was nothing, really.
                              STEVE
It wasn't "nothing," Roger. It was really something. It
was something to me. Our relationship adds up to a
whole bunch of something's for me. So…based on all
those something's, I have decided to give you one
more chance. I think, if we try, we can put this affair
behind us.
                              ROGER
                     (Immediately excited.)
You mean you forgive me?
                              STEVE
                        (Still calm.)
Ah, ah, ah. Not so fast, space cowboy. I said I'd give
you a chance. I didn't say I'd forgiven you yet.
                              ROGER
            (His excitement giving way to confusion.)
What…What do you mean?
                              STEVE
They're bringing the dogs out onto the track for the
third race right now. The third race, Roger. Our race.
                              ROGER
And…
                              STEVE
It's simple, really. I placed a bet this morning on a
pastime I know nothing about. I placed that bet, and I
am here at this place, based solely on my faith in you.
During the course of this day, that faith has been
seriously challenged. The race is your way of making
it up to me. If our dog wins, you and I will go to

                              58

Theresa and try to work this out, and no matter what happens with me and Theresa, you and I will still be cool. But, if Keep the Faith loses…we go our separate ways, and never speak to each other again.

ROGER

You're kidding, right?

(STEVE remains constant. Unmoved. ROGER stands up.)

You can't be serious, Steve! You can't put the weight of our whole relationship on the four legs of a dog! This is ridiculous! I don't accept the bet. I don't accept this.

STEVE

It's not a negotiable offer, Roger. This is the only chance you get. If you don't accept it, you start walking now, chump. This race…This is your only avenue back into my life.

ROGER

The only avenue…This is what you say to me? The only avenue?

(He's exhausted. He finally accepts.)

Alright, then. If it's the only choice I've got…But I'd just like to go on record as to my total disagreement towards this whole thing.

STEVE

Your objection is so noted. Now shut-up, they're about to start.

(They are both sitting on the bench. STEVE is calm, not even looking at the track. He's reading the Racing Form. ROGER tries to sit calmly, but he's fidgeting.

The Loudspeaker announces "And they're off!"
ROGER immediately jumps from the bench and runs to the rail of the track.)

ROGER

(He jumps and yells wildly at the dogs.)

Come on Number 9! Come on, Keep the Faith! Come on, baby!

(He takes off his sports coat and uses it in a whipping motion.)
Faster, baby, faster! Go, dog, go! Move, you damn fleabag!
(He looks back at STEVE who is simply sitting on the bench staring at him. ROGER then turns back to the race.)
Oh, God! He's neck and neck with Number 4! Come on, baby! Run your damn legs off!
(He throws his jacket to the ground.)
They're almost at the finish line! Turn up the juice, baby! Don't fail me now!
(At the time that all the dogs would have passed the finish line, ROGER jumps up and runs around, unsure of the final outcome.)
Who won? Who won?
(He grabs a random on-looker and asks him.)
Who won?

JOE
Too close to tell. It was either the 9 or the 4. 4 looked like he had the edge, though.

ROGER
What the hell do you know?
(He is still frantically looking for the outcome.)
Who the hell won the damn race!
(The Loudspeaker announces "And the winner of the third race…" There is a long pause before the announcement goes through. ROGER screams at the loudspeaker.)
Who?
(The Loudspeaker then finally says "…Number 9, Keep the Faith." ROGER laughs out loud in jubilation and relief, and then falls to his knees in exhaustion. He is sweating profusely and has dirt on his pants when he gets up. He walks over to where his jacket has been thrown and picks it up off the ground and dusts it off, still laughing as he puts it on. ROGER then looks at

*STEVE, still sitting back on the bench, looking at
ROGER, looking very stern. ROGER suspects a
doublecross.)*
ROGER
(In disbelief.)
Don't you look at me like that, damn it! A deal's a
deal! You have to forgive me.
*(After a long pause, STEVE's stern look turns to a
smile, and he reaches his hand out to ROGER.)*
STEVE
(In a calm voice.)
Let's collect our winnings.
*(ROGER laughs out loud at this line and grabs STEVE
toward him and gives him a big hug.)*
ROGER
I knew you'd come around.
STEVE
I am such a pushover.
ROGER
That's why we're such good friends.
*(They pull away from the big hug, but are still holding
each other as STEVE looks ROGER up and down.)*
STEVE
Damn, son. You're a stinky, sweaty mess.
ROGER
Well, it's not like you put any pressure on me or
anything.
STEVE
Well, what the hell are we standing around here for?
Let's go collect our money, eh?
ROGER
Hey, buddy, I'm with you. But…uh…what do we do
after that?
STEVE
Just what I said. We'll go to Theresa and straighten out
the whole thing.

ROGER
And…divorce proceedings?
STEVE
I may have been hasty to mention those. I have to see
how Theresa reacts, but I still love my wife, Roger, so
it should work out fine.
ROGER
All you need is love, you know.
STEVE
Thanks, John. Does that make me Ringo?
ROGER
I guess you can be Paul if you want.
*(They laugh and start to walk off. STEVE puts his
hands in his pockets, looking up at the sky.)*
STEVE
And, of course, you will have to tell Angela.
*(STEVE keeps walking but ROGER stops as soon as
STEVE says Angela's name.)*
ROGER
(Looking out at the audience.)
Tell Angela?
*(He then chases after STEVE, catching him just before
he leaves the stage.)*
Hey, Steve, can we talk about that?
STEVE
(After a pause, putting his arm over his shoulder.)
You are so whipped.
*(They walk offstage and ROGER still wears a worried
face. The lights fade and we are done.)*

END SCENE 5
CURTAIN

Two for Smoking

A Play in Two Acts

Jeremey W. Gingrich

<u>Two for Smoking</u>

A Play in Two Acts

AJ Mitchell and Chris Malone are bookmakers in Florida. They have been friends for years, since college, and they are relentless bachelors and adamant smokers. Their greatest bonding times are when they go out to dinner, which they never have to pay for since their clients always want to keep them happy, and the restaurant owners they know all love to gamble. The overwhelming quality these two possess is their inability to keep out of other people's business, and to continually smoke while they do it. Like most men who have found a formula that works for them, any change to their daily routine is seen as a catastrophe. This chronicles a method AJ and Chris used when one such catastrophe arose.

Jeremey W. Gingrich

Time: Present

Synopsis of Scenes

ACT ONE
SCENE 1—The Italian Restaurant

SCENE 2—The Chinese Restaurant

ACT TWO
SCENE 1—The All-Night Diner

SCENE 2—The Alamo

Act One

Scene 1- *The Italian Restaurant. AJ and Chris enter the restaurant wearing suits, AJ has a bow tie untied hanging around his neck, and Chris's tie is loose on his neck. They walk up to the "Please Wait to be Seated" table where the owner stands, their table is a booth set up stage right. There are tables set up beside their booth where people are already sitting, but they are only heard and focused upon when they become relevant to the story.*

CHRIS
(As they walk through the doors)

Fleas?

AJ

Fleas. Must be thousands of 'em.

CHRIS

You don't even own a fish, how did you get fleas?

AJ

I didn't get fleas, alright? My apartment has fleas. And how does anybody? They just migrate?

CHRIS

You gonna start a circus?

AJ

Oh, that's golden. I'm dying' over here.

GINO
(GINO is the restaurant owner who is a client of AJ)

Ah, my good friend, I believe you have something for me. And Mr. Malone, it's good to see you as well.

CHRIS

Hey, Gino.

AJ
(Walks up to GINO, shakes his hand and reaches in his inside pocket with the other, he pulls out an envelope and hands it to GINO)

I gotta hand it to ya, Gino. Going' long on Tampa Bay over the Colts…it was a pretty ballsy move.

67

GINO
(Putting the envelope in his inside pocket)
Sometimes you get lucky. You staying to dine or is this all business?

AJ
Actually, we were hoping to maybe eat some good food tonight, but since we're here…

GINO
Always with the insults, and I always treat you so good. Tonight, I swear I will do terrible things to your soup. Smoking, of course.
(Grabs two menus and starts walking through the restaurant.)

AJ
(Following GINO through the restaurant)
Well, in that case I'll stick with the salad. Big game this Saturday, Gino. Florida/Florida State is always a barn-burner.

CHRIS
…And one hell of a headache for us.

AJ
What's the matter, baby boy, you afraid of people handing you their money? This Saturday is a major payday.

CHRIS
You know me, AJ. I hate working with people I don't know. I have a set number of clients, and we have a great relationship. These big games bring out every crackpot and their mother trying' to place bets with me. I blame my sterling reputation.

AJ
(Now they're at their table, past the non-smoking section)
Or maybe it's because you write your number on bathroom stalls.

CHRIS
Hey, you can't pay for that kind of advertising.

GINO

Here ya go, fellas. Table for two, and I know you like
booths. Sammy's gonna be your waiter and he should
be here shortly for your drinks.
(Leaning in to AJ)
And I'll call you by the end of the week with my
wager. Right now I'm thinking Gators, but I haven't
done my research. Enjoy the meal.
(He leaves)

AJ

Talk to ya later, Gino.
(When GINO is gone)
I love when people do "research." It makes taking their
money so much easier.

CHRIS

So what are you gonna do about your flea problem?

AJ

My what? Oh, the super said he can't get someone in
to take care of 'em till next Tuesday, so until then I'm
gonna set up some of those flea bomb things around
the apartment.
*(AJ notices a man in a small table next to his getting
up to leave. As he gets up, he puts his jacket over his
arm and his wallet falls out of the inside pocket.)*
So I might have to stay with you a couple of nights.
*(AJ says this line slowly as he gets up slowly to take off
his jacket and go get the wallet.)*

CHRIS

That's fine...
(Notices AJ getting up)
Where...
(As AJ picks up the wallet)
Did...Did that guy just drop that?

AJ
(Rifling through the wallet)
Yeah. Hey, cute kids.

69

CHRIS

What are you doing?

AJ

Relax, I'm just checking' some things out, that's all.
(Sees the money in the bill portion of the wallet and pulls out 3 20's.)
Hey, hey... Who's up for a bottle of wine, eh?

CHRIS

(Grabbing the wallet and money from AJ's hands)
Give me that.
(He puts the bills back in the wallet and closes it.)
You're unbelievable sometimes, you know that?
(He gets up to run after the guy.)

AJ

(Snatching the wallet back)
Now hold on a minute, will ya? Just sit down, sit down
a second here.
(Chris sits down glaring at AJ)
Now, before you go running after this guy, maybe we
ought to do a quick overview of the situation here...
(Thinking hard, stalling and stuttering)
We don't... This... This wallet may not even belong to
that particular gentleman... How are we to know?

CHRIS

What?

AJ

(Fiddles through the wallet and pulls out the driver's license)
Look, Look at this, it doesn't even look anything like
that guy.

CHRIS

You didn't even get a good look at him, you saw him
for 15 seconds tops.

AJ

No, no I'm good with faces, Chris. This wallet does
not belong to that man. He probably found it himself

somewhere, or…you know what, he might have picked this poor chumps pocket.

(Pointing to the face in the driver's license.)

He had those shifty eyes, you know. Who knows how much money was in here originally? And you want to give it back to him?

CHRIS

I'm not having this conversation.

(He grabs the wallet and puts the driver's license back in it.)

And now, I have to run.

(Running off)

Watch my jacket.

AJ

(Calling after him loudly)

If you facilitate crime you become part of the problem. Damn, I hate the idea of losing free money.

(Lighting a cigarette)

And I can't help but smile when I benefit from someone else's misfortune…a kind of bonus that comes with the job. You know, another thing that has always made me smile has been the song "It's my party." Not that I've ever been that big a fan of Leslie Gore, and that teeny bopper bubble gum bullshit might have been the worst thing to happen to music, but it's the lyrics, the story behind the song that gives me a grin. No matter what anybody tries to tell you about music, lyrics make the song. Granted, Leslie went a little crazy with repetition in her song…the whole "cry if I want to" thing…but through closer inspection of the main storyline, you'll find a very interesting set of events. First, you've got this girl, probably one of these rich girl debutants, having a birthday party, a typical celebration for herself, and she's all upset. Why? Because her trophy boyfriend is with some other girl. Nothing new about that, but this is the kicker…This is what floats my boat. It's this girl's birthday party, and

Johnny, her boyfriend, knows that all her friends are there and knows that something as obvious as him leaving her for another girl is going to be embarrassing and humiliating, but does he let that stop him? No! He drops the uppity bitch for what I like to think is a sweeter piece of ass, to put it delicately. You gotta admire the chops on a guy like that.

(Drags his cigarette)
(CHRIS walks back onstage out of breath. Panting)

AJ

Jesus, how far did you have to run?

CHRIS

He had only gotten about a block away. Jeez, I'm out of shape. I could've sprinted twice that distance in college, no problem. Must be getting older.

(As he sits down he lights a cigarette)

The body's the first thing to go, y' know.

AJ

Yeah, it's a cryin' shame. So are you happy, you did your good deed for the day.

CHRIS

Yes, as a matter of fact I am.

(While AJ drags his cigarette he continually blows the smoke towards the non-smoking section.)

And as a matter of fact...

(Pulls a $20 out of his pocket)

...I got a reward.

AJ

You know, technically I found the wallet. Shouldn't that reward be mine? I mean if you're so hell-bent on being an upstanding citizen, isn't that 20 rightfully mine?

CHRIS

(The waiter, SAMMY, comes up as they're talking)

I'm gonna pretend you didn't say that.

AJ

(To SAMMY)

72

Hey, Sammy, what's happening'?
                    SAMMY
Not much, AJ. Heard Gino did well last weekend. You
slipping' or what?
                    AJ
Hey, don't worry about me, I'll make it back before
you know it. So what are we having', Honest Abe?
Wine or the hard stuff?
                    CHRIS
What is the social convention for Italian food, anyway?
I know it's white for fish, red for steak so...for
pasta...what? A blush?
                    AJ
Sounds good. Sammy, could we get a bottle of White
Zinfandel and lots of bread...I mean keeps it coming.
Pile it on.
                    SAMMY
Of course. Be right back.
                (Walks off)
*(AJ laughs to himself as he drags his cigarette and
blows the smoke towards the non-smoking section.)*
                    CHRIS
            (Shaking his head)
Why does Gino always put us at this table? I hate when
you do that.
                    AJ
I told him I like this table. I love this.
*(He drags again and blows his smoke towards the non-
                smoking section.)*
Ha Ha suck it up, losers. I give 'em five minutes before
they complain to their waiter.
            (Imitating a whiny non-smoker)
"Excuse me, sir. But the evil smokers are ruining my
dinner." Then the waiter will come over and ask us to
watch the smoke or whatever, and we'll look like the
bad guys.

73

CHRIS

Then you'll blow more smoke at them.

AJ

Well, they asked for it. Besides, it's cool being the bad guy.

CHRIS

Is that what you want to be when you grow up?

AJ

Don't have sympathy for these people, Chris. Make no mistake, there is a war going on.

(The waiter brings the bottle of wine and bread while AJ is talking. Chris mutters a quiet "Thank you" but AJ keeps talking.)

And we are losing. Look at what has happened to the smoking society in recent years. All the non-smoking propaganda, the death of Joe Camel, hell the entire state of California. Those scowls we get from people as we walk through the non-smoking section to smoking are not because of your aftershave. These people see us as stupid and weak, victims of a lack of self-restraint or as helpless addicts to rival the average homeless heroin junkie. And what's worse, we have no method of retaliation. Smoking ads are not allowed on television, hardly any of Hollywood's leading men smoke anymore. I'm tellin' you we're a dyin' breed.

CHRIS

(Looking at his cigarette)

And we're dying because of the cigarettes.

AJ

Judas! Don't believe the hype, man. Be proud of the habit. We're all gonna die, just smokers will look that much cooler when we go. We even have our own unique language, almost foreign to the infidel outsiders. Watch this.

(He gets the attention of a man sitting with his friend at a two person table next to theirs. He is a FAT MAN,

*wearing a shirt and tie and taking a drag of his
cigarette.)*
Excuse me, sir.
*(FAT MAN turns his attention towards AJ, the lights
come up brighter on FAT MAN's table, further stage
right, to the front of the stage.)*
FAT MAN
Yes?
AJ
Marlboro?
FAT MAN
Camels.
AJ
Menthol?
FAT MAN
Unfiltered.
AJ
How long?
FAT MAN
24 years, no sign of stopping.
AJ
Excellent.
(Now to FAT MAN's friend)
And you, sir?
*(As he asks, the guy, SHY GUY, sulks and sort of
cowers away from him.)*
FAT MAN
You'll have to excuse my friend…
(Leaning in to AJ)
He's tryin' to quit.
(AJ's face becomes stern)
Wife's orders.
AJ
Nobody likes a quitter, friend.
(SHY GUY looks up finally)
SHY GUY
It gets worse.

(He lifts up his sleeve and shows the two a nicotine patch on his arm. As he does, AJ screams in surprise gets up, takes the patch off his arm and throws it on the ground, stomping on it.)

AJ

(After looking around, noticing he's making a scene)
Sorry.
(He looks down at SHY GUY and offers a cigarette from his pack. SHY GUY takes it, half out of fear. AJ then puts the pack away as CHRIS bends in to light the cigarette. They all take a long drag together and exhale at the same time.)
Isn't it great that we're all smoking?

SHY GUY

My wife's gonna kill me.

AJ

Ah, but what a way to go.
(He sits back down and drinks his wine. CHRIS is buttering a piece of bread.)

CHRIS

I think we have maybe five more minutes before they kick us out of here.

AJ

You say that every time we go out.

CHRIS

That's because every time we go out it becomes a recruiting trip for you to enlist all smokers who cross our path into this war of yours. A sort of "us against them" group of smokers vs. non-smokers, so you can play the part of field general. A sort of George Patton meets the Marlboro Man.
(AJ eats some bread.)

AJ

That's a new one, General Patton and the Marlboro Man. I believe I like that.
(SAMMY comes back up to get their order.)

SAMMY

So what's it gonna be tonight, fellas?

AJ

Chicken or Veal? What do you think?

CHRIS

Let's go with veal. Parmigian or Marsala?

AJ

Parmigian. Calamari?

CHRIS

Definitely.

(They look at SAMMY as if they've already ordered to make sure he's got the order.)

SAMMY

You guys are worse than a married couple. So, to make sure I deciphered the code correctly, you got a Calamari appetizer comin' to ya before Veal Parmigian, is that right?

CHRIS

Exactly.

SAMMY

And the wine?

AJ

It's fine.

(SAMMY nods and leaves. As he does, FAT MAN and SHY GUY pay their bill and get up to leave.)

FAT MAN

Well, friend, best of luck in your efforts against the enemy.

AJ

We're all in this together.

FAT MAN

So be it. See you on the battleground.

(FAT MAN gives a slight salute.)

AJ

As you were.

(As they leave, AJ returns the salute. SHY GUY leans down to talk to AJ)

SHY GUY

Could I get one more...for the road?

AJ

(Getting one out of his pack.)

That's a good soldier.

(Gives him a cigarette and he leaves.)

CHRIS

His wife's gonna kill him.

(SAMMY comes to the table after the men leave and cleans the table. AJ watches him. CHRIS notices that AJ is watching the table.)

CHRIS

Looking for another wallet?

AJ

No! But if I find one I'll be sure to tell you about it.

CHRIS

Ooh there's some animosity in that, my friend.

AJ

Observant, aren't ya?

CHRIS

Don't worry, AJ. I will drag you kicking and screaming towards honest living.

AJ

Bully for me.

(He drinks his wine.)

Hey...

(Something has just donned on him.)

...you know what I just remembered?

CHRIS

(Eating bread)

What?

AJ

Junior year at Faber, when we put together that little bake sale at the Students Center.

(They both laugh)

What did we say it was for again?

CHRIS
(Thinking)
Ah, shit. We said it was for…We said we worked for
the people at Jerry's kids.
(They both say Jerry's Kids at the same time.)
The Jerry Lewis thing.

AJ
We were up till 4 the night before baking those
cookies, what'd we make like 18 batches on that one
cookie sheet?

CHRIS
I still say we should've bought more supplies.

AJ
I remember we burnt a batch and almost our whole
kitchen when we left that batch in the oven and fell
asleep…what around 2:30?

CHRIS
Still made quite a few, though. We cleared more than
300 dollars off that little scam. I don't know why we
didn't do it more often.

AJ
And who was the one who came up with that brilliant
scheme? Who was the one who, one lazy Sunday
afternoon, said "Hey, I've got an idea!"
(Leans in)
Who is the mastermind who formulated the intricate
plan to steal charity money from retarded children?
*(As they talk, GINO seats a man at the table that FAT
MAN and SHY GUY were at. The man, RICH,
whispers something to GINO who nods as he pulls the
chair out for RICH, who has a manila envelope, and
then GINO leaves. RICH takes off his jacket and puts it
on the back of his chair. GINO comes back with an
uncorked bottle of wine. RICH sits down at his table
and pours his wine as the conversation takes place)*

CHRIS

Hey, first of all, we didn't steal anything from
anybody, we were not thieves, we were fund raisers.
The funds just happened to be raised for a different
charity than the people thought. And second, Jerry's
kids are not retarded, alright, they have muscular
dystrophy. You see, that's why I had to do all the
talking for the fund raiser…

AJ

And you want to drag me towards honest living?
(SAMMY brings the calamari to the table)

CHRIS

Perhaps I've seen the error of my ways…
*(Sees RICH at his table, watches him as he looks down
at his envelope and downs an entire glass of wine.
CHRIS is puzzled but continues talking.)*
Perhaps I've undergone a period of personal growth.
*(RICH pours another glass of wine and then pulls a
flask out of his pocket.)*

AJ

Personal growth?!?
*(CHRIS shushes AJ and motions toward RICH. They
watch as he pours some of the contents of the flask into
his glass of wine, and drinks the wine in one big gulp
again. He then pulls out the manila envelope.)*

CHRIS

*(Pulls out his wallet and takes a $20 out and puts it on
the table.)*
20 says he just got fired.
(Thinking)
From a job he held for no less than 10 years.

AJ

You want to do this again? You know I've won the last
4.

CHRIS

I figure I'm due.

AJ
(Pulls out a 20)
You're on. I know it's a woman. Woman problems.
Rejected by a girlfriend or left by his wife. This is win
number 5, I know it.

CHRIS
We'll see.
*(They get up and walk over to RICH's table. Rich has
poured another glass of wine and has pulled out a
cigarette, CHRIS lights it.)*

CHRIS
Take it easy, buddy. You're about to depress the whole
restaurant.

RICH
(Surprised)
What?

AJ
What seems to be the problem, pal? We're about two
seconds away from taking your belt and shoelaces.

RICH
(Still surprised)
Sorry. Just…uh…just got some bad news, that's all.
I'm not…not handling it as well as I should.

CHRIS
What kind of news? Like…problems at work? I mean,
everyone has problems at work.

RICH
No, it's just…
(He pulls out his papers from the manila envelope)
My wife…we've been separated for 2 months now,
and…I just got served the papers today. It's official.
I'm a statistic.
*(AJ smiles and picks up the money from the table and
he sits down and drinks wine. CHRIS is still standing.)*

CHRIS
*(Looking back and forth between RICH and AJ,
looking for AJ to help.)*

What…How long…Were you married long? No, wait a minute, don't answer that. Jesus, I don't even know your frickin' name.

CENTER RICH

It's Rich. It'll be 14 years this May. Julia insisted on a May wedding. June was too obvious. Almost everyone at the wedding wished us well, but said we were too young. Maybe we were. My parents said we were months before but I knew better.

(Slight laugh)

Never argue with your parents. She was the love of my life. I knew I wanted to be with her the rest of my life…

(Verge of tears.)

…and now…

(Holding up the papers.)

(CHRIS fidgets around and looks to AJ for help. AJ is smiling and putting his 40 dollars in his wallet.)

CHRIS

(To AJ under his breath)

What should we do? We should do something.

(AJ shrugs his shoulders in an "I don't know" motion.)

CHRIS

What brought upon…what…why? Why'd she leave? Was it for another guy…or was it one of those things where she was trying to find herself?

AJ

(From the table)

Probably trying to find herself with another guy.

RICH

Hey, I'm right here, you know. She left me for my best friend.

AJ

That's why I made sure my best friend was thoroughly unattractive.

CHRIS

(CHRIS glares back at him.)

You know you really aren't helping here.

AJ

(Getting up)

You want help. This is help.

*(He walks over to RICH and picks up the divorce
papers. He then talks to RICH.)*

You see these. These are not divorce papers. Sure, they
look like divorce papers, and they do in fact signify
your horrible and embarrassing failure of a marriage.
But the hidden fact is that these papers signify your
liberation.

(CHRIS buries his head in his hands.)

RICH

Liberation?

AJ

That's exactly right. And right now you should feel
born again. These papers give you a life you've only
dreamt about. You're what...thirty-five, thirty-six?

RICH

Thirty-five.

AJ

Hey, alright, just like us. Jeez, I hate seeing guys like
you...in your condition. You're like a dog who's been
on a leash all his life and then when his master takes
him out in a field and lets him go, he doesn't know
what to do. The poor dog weeps uncontrollably, a
pathetic display of a lack of independence. You see, all
this time you've been married you've had limited
movement, hence the leash analogy. Your dreams and
passions have been hindered by your wife. They are
called the "ball and chain" for a reason my friend. And
now you've been released. They threaten you with
"Till death do you part," but you've gotten early
parole. Rejoice!

CHRIS

This is not the time for this particular discussion.

RICH

Time for what?

CHRIS

See, we sort of have a particular lifestyle choice which works for us. We have worked on it for years, and we're at a great place now. However…

(More to AJ than RICH)

…since we are sensitive individuals who are sympathetic to the normal human condition, we realize that this is not a lifestyle fit for everyone, and we certainly do not wish to push our unique lifestyle on anybody else.

RICH

Lifestyle? Oh, great. I need help and advice on women and marriage and I get a couple of Liberace's.

AJ

Relax, it's not like that, he's just my best friend since college. A liability mostly, but I keep him around for comic relief. Anyway, this is the perfect time for this discussion. And it happens to be in our particular field of expertise.

RICH

You guys counselors or psychiatrists or something?

CHRIS

Actually, we're bookmakers.

AJ

Bookies, C. Alright, we are bookies. You always want to use the official term, like we're accountants or something.

RICH

You're bookies? Jesus, fellas, I'm not asking for advice on the Laker game here! And you went to college for this?

CHRIS

Well, you ain't gotta say it like that. We went to college for the same reason everyone does…to drink. Besides, if it wasn't for college, I never would've met

84

this bozo, and if I didn't meet him, I wouldn't have
met his uncle, and if I hadn't met his uncle, I would
never have gotten a job as a bookie in his organization.

AJ

What is this, plot summary? We're getting off track
here. Our friend Rick here...

RICH

Rich.

AJ

Whatever. The point is...Our friend has been hurt by a
woman. Why? Because he thought he needed her. And
Jesus for what?

RICH
(Pause)

Love?

*(CHRIS touches RICH on the arm and makes a
hushing face to him)*

AJ

Love. What a joke. Love's the biggest scam since the
pet rock.

RICH

That's funny, I bought four of those. Named 'em after
the Beatles.

AJ

The need for love is a public illusion. And one that is
perpetuated everywhere. Love's got the best press
agents and PR people working on its behalf. All the
best songs are written about it. The greatest movies of
all time are focused around it...

CHRIS

I assure you there's a point here somewhere.

AJ

And a damn good one.
(Picking up the papers again.)
These papers signify your realization of that illusion.
And they give you a chance to try your life without it.

For instance, what do you do? And not your job, I
mean what do you like to do?
(He speaks in an Al Capone accent.)
Your enthusiasms. What is that which brings you joy.
RICH
(Looking inward. Deeply trying not to remember.)
We used to go to the beach on Sunday morning…
AJ
Not what you and…
(Searching for her name.)
CHRIS
Julia.
AJ
Not what you two used to do together. I mean when it
was just you, even before you were married. You did
exist before that day, didn't you?
RICH
I was into movies. All up through college I'd collect
movie posters and various movie memorabilia. When I
had more money in pocket, I got some cooler stuff.
One of my favorite things was actually a Jimmy
Stewart autographed script from "Harvey," one of my
favorite movies, by far.
AJ
Where's the script now?
RICH
I have…It's in a small box in my closet, next to Gene
Kelly's tap shoes.
CHRIS
You bought Gene Kelly's taps? Where? How?
RICH
There was an auction down in Miami one day. I took a
day off and went down and bid on everything I could.
Most of the really good stuff was too expensive.
Somebody bought De Niro's gun from "Taxi Driver"
for $7000 dollars. Some drug dealer was obviously a
big fan. Oh, and the box of chocolates from "Forrest

Gump" went for something like five grand. Man, I wanted that. But I managed to outlast the suckers and get the tap shoes Gene Kelly used in "American in Paris." I bought a display case and a little plaque for display purposes...I figured it would make for a good conversation piece.

                          AJ
And it's in the closet.

                        CHRIS
Jesus, Rich, I wish you could've seen your face when you were talking about that stuff. You lit up like a kid in a candy store. One might even say you were giddy.

                          AJ
But Julia didn't like that stuff, right? So into the closet it goes. And how many of those movie posters hung in your place when you were married?
              (RICH shakes his head no.)
None. Big surprise. See, that's another thing about marriage...everybody says it's a compromise, like that's an excuse for the hardships. You were probably real upset when the tap shoes were exiled to the closet. But, all the marriage consultants and relationship experts can say is, "Hey, marriage means compromise." Which means somebody has to settle. I say, never settle. I say, compromise is just a bullshit word meaning, "deal with unhappiness," and life's too short to be unhappy.

                        CHRIS
What my friend is trying to say is...well look at us. We hang whatever we want on our walls. If I wanted to buy the box of chocolates from "Forrest Gump," I could, no matter how much it cost. I wouldn't have to discuss it with anyone. I do whatever I want, whenever I want and with whomever I want.

                          AJ
Yeah, that's another thing. How much time did you get to hang out with your friends when you were married?

RICH

Obviously not enough, since my best friend had the
time to steal my wife away from me.

AJ

Ah, screw him. Backstabbing bastard. He deserves
what he gets.

RICH

He's getting my wife.

AJ

Well, let the punishment fit the crime.

CHRIS

The point is now you can spend as much time with guy
friends, doing guy stuff, as long as you want. You
don't have to keep looking at the clock, or call home to
tell the wife where you are and how late you'll be…or
to ask permission to stay out later.

AJ
(Disgusted)

Ask permission. Man, nothing pisses me off more than
the sight of a grown man asking if he is allowed to stay
out with his buddies just a little while longer. I haven't
done that since I was 25…and the woman was my
mother.

RICH

Wait, 25? Why…

CHRIS
*(Interrupting RICH and kind of hushing him, saying
low.)*

He was one of those guys, you know, hard time
cutting' the cord.
(RICH shakes his head in understanding.)

AJ

Hey, it wasn't like that, alright. My mother just…This
is not about me!

RICH

I know, I know. I get it. It's just…When guys like me
make that call…When we ask for "permission," sure

we sound meek, sure we look whipped, but you'll always see a little smile creep across our faces. Because we know that on the other end of that phone is someone who cares about us, and we want them to know that we're alright. Just as I am sure you did with your mother.

(CHRIS taps his arm and shakes his head.)

Furthermore, the person on the other end of that phone is genuinely sad that we will not be home to spend time with them, and that makes us smile as well. And now...

(RICH takes the papers from AJ)

...that's all over.

(Temper and voice rising.)

And sure, tonight I can go home and put all my movie posters up. La De Da. And I can go crazy with my Gene Kelly taps and "Harvey" script. Whoop de do. But, the fact is, I don't want to spend any time in my own house anymore. I can't stand to set foot in that big empty place because that person...that person I would call for permission...that person who I thought would always be there...she isn't there anymore. And I wish I could tell...I wish I could explain or describe how painful that is.

(There is a long and uncomfortable silence as RICH just sits there with the papers.)

AJ

You know, maybe the wine's not such a bad idea.

(He drinks from RICH's glass.)

(SAMMY comes back onstage with plates and the Chicken Parmigian. He places it down on the table, and looks for a second at the guys in their situation. Shakes his head, then exits.)

CHRIS

(Getting up and walking around RICH)

You know, this is kind of funny.

AJ

Yeah, Chris. Hilarious.
(Back at his table dishing his food onto his plate.)
You know our food's here now.

CHRIS

No, listen. You said you got married at what?

RICH

21. Why?

CHRIS

Married at 21, you'd been together for most of your youth, right? High school and shit?

RICH

Yeah.

CHRIS

(Puts his head back in a big laugh.)
And you're upset?

RICH

Upset? My world is coming down around me. I'm about two seconds away from bursting into tears in front of total strangers…What do you think? And that fucking laugh is helping the anger just a bit.

CHRIS

Right now you're upset because you feel alone, right? Like you'll be alone forever?

RICH

It doesn't happen twice.

AJ

Hey, she ran off with your best friend, are you really sure it happened once?

CHRIS

Ha, you've got it easy.

RICH

(Getting real upset)
Have you been listening? I feel like I'm dying here! What the hell is so easy about that?

90

AJ
Chris, maybe we ought to be getting back to our table now, eh? Rich here seems to be getting irate and there are knives present.

CHRIS
Let me tell you something, Rich, all these feelings of loneliness and rejection, the fear of being alone…I've felt them before. For nine years. Nine years! From my years after high school all up through college, and the years following I couldn't get a woman to save my fucking life. Your big problem is going home to an empty house, well, welcome to my world, partner. I did that every night for nine years, wondering what I was doing wrong. Was it the way I walked, the way I dressed, acted, looked, spoke…anything. Brainwashed, I kept thinking the natural order was for a man to be with a woman, and if women were so inclined to stay away from me, there must be something horribly wrong with me. And that was my mentality for nine years. And let me tell you something, friend, I tried everything. I tried meeting women in singles bars, the grocery store, the library…I even joined a health club. And through these many years, the longest relationship I had was 7 months, thanks to the health club. Her name was Rebecca, blonde, tight body…she ended up leaving me for the aerobics instructor…Dominique. Ever been left for a woman, Rich? Pretty fuckin' hard to wake up the next morning. Let me tell ya.

AJ
Makes for a great story though.

CHRIS
(Not even paying any attention)
Oh, but that's not the best part.
(He laughs to himself.)
Get this, when I was 25, I was desperate. I did something I swore I would never do. I started going to dance clubs. Sure, I know what you're thinking,

91

"What's wrong with dance clubs?" But let me assure you there is something very wrong. Very, very wrong. Ever been?

RICH

No.

AJ

Of course not, you were married.

RICH

No, I just don't dance.

CHRIS

Neither does anyone at a dance club, man. It's just 800 people on 8 square-feet of dance floor grinding up against each other. And sure, that feels pretty cool, 'cause sometimes you end up grinding on a rather nice looking young lady. Of course, she's 17 at the most, so you feel like a child-molester. Which would make a man leave, right? The average 25-year old should realize he's making an ass of himself and never go back, right? But that's why dance clubs are always packed, Rich. They develop some kind of mental hold on people, and you go back again and again and you just can't stop. It takes hold, and it starts to change you. I was buying tight sparkling shirts, puttin' mousse in my hair, dousing myself in cologne…Hell, I even bought a pair of leather pants. These legs, in leather pants!

AJ

You never told me about those.

CHRIS

And let us never mention them again. Jesus, Rich I would even buy dance music CD's so I could practice moves at home.

(He breaks down at the table.)

Practice at home.

(Puts head down.)

AJ
(Puts his hands on CHRIS's shoulders comforting him.)
Ever see a grown man practicing the Macarena in the privacy of his own home? Not a pretty sight.

RICH
But didn't you ever meet any women at these clubs? Once you "grind" on someone, I'd imagine you can't just casually part ways.

CHRIS
You'd be surprised. But with the women I would meet at these clubs, the occasional 18 year old, whenever we'd go out, she'd just want to go dancing again…and the vicious cycle continued. I even had to go to a support group to break the habit. I'm a sponsor now. But the point of this whole thing is to show you what you missed. You missed out on the pain and humiliation of the hunt. So…
(Picks up the divorce papers)
…when you hand these to Julia, even though she hurt you, thank her with all of your heart for saving you from this hell.

RICH
But those feelings of rejection and isolation…those are what I'm feeling now. Are these the feelings I have to look forward to until I find a woman again? That could take forever.

AJ
It doesn't work that way. And what do you want another woman for anyway? You know, insanity is defined as doing the same thing over and over and expecting a different result.

RICH
Then when will it end? How do you make it stop?

CHRIS
I just started listening to him.
(Points to AJ)

He had been telling me for years and I finally started listening. He kept explaining to me that I didn't need a woman in my life, and how the humiliation I was facing while trying to get a woman would only be surpassed by the degradation I would experience if I actually got one.

RICH

So, what like you're off women?

CHRIS

That's the lifestyle we were talking about. And sure, it's different, and like I said, not for everyone, but in your case, at this point in your life…If I were you I'd consider it. Sure, we're still physically attracted to women…but that's what strip clubs are for. Instant nudity, no compromises.

RICH

I can't go to strip clubs. I never know what to look at. If I look at their eyes, I feel like some psycho stalker, and if I look at their breasts or whatever…I feel like a pervert. So I end up paying a $15 dollar cover charge to stare at the floor.

AJ

Then perhaps a vast pornographic library?

RICH

I don't even own one now.

CHRIS

Really? Not any?

RICH

We had cable.

AJ

Cable?! Soft-core shit.
(Pulls out a card from his wallet.)
You need to get a hold of this guy…Harry Zimm. He owns this store on 23rd and Mercury.

RICH
(Reading the card.)
"Different Strokes?"

AJ

Tell him AJ sent ya, he'll hook ya right up. Just remember the best women in the world are two-dimensional.

RICH

So is this how you cope with the frustration? Just eat out, drink and bother innocent bystanders.

CHRIS

Pretty much. The main thing is to find a friend, one you can trust, and spend all your time with him.

AJ

Granted, you might not find a friend as supportive or nurturing or even as cool as me, but the important thing is to try. And for God's sake, if you remember only one thing we said here tonight, remember this. There's only one woman you really need in your life, and you left her when you were 25.

RICH

Actually, I moved out when…

AJ

You left her when you were 25.

RICH

Well, I'm not gonna lie, it still hurts. But I think with a few years of intense therapy, I should be ready to enter society.

AJ

You want the best therapy. Come here.
(He pulls RICH towards the edge of the smoking section. He motions CHRIS over.)
You gotta do it too.

CHRIS

Alright. For Rich.

AJ

(To RICH)
Now watch and follow my lead.
(AJ takes a big drag of his cigarette and so does CHRIS. RICH catches on and drags big as well. They

all blow it out into the non-smoking section. They
laugh as coughs come from offstage.)

AJ

I swear to God I could do this all day.

RICH

I can see how a person could derive quite a bit of
pleasure from a pastime like that.

AJ

Your prescription calls for two or three times a week
of doing stuff like that. Have a little "me" time.
You've earned it.

CHRIS

Here, here.

RICH

Maybe you're right, but it all sounds too simple. I'll
give it a shot, I guess.

(He goes to his jacket, which is on his chair and pulls
out his wallet, takes a twenty out of the wallet and puts
it on the table. He then puts the wallet back in his
inside pocket while holding his jacket. He then puts the
jacket over his arm and his wallet falls out, unseen by
CHRIS, but AJ sees it.)

If you'll excuse me gentlemen, I have some posters to
hang.

(As he leaves he shakes AJ's hand first, then as he
shakes hands with CHRIS, AJ sneaks over to the wallet
and rifles through it as RICH and CHRIS talk.)

I won't lie to you, I will probably never be truly
comfortable without a woman by my side, but I thank
you for the different perspective.

CHRIS

Best of luck, Rich. Like I said, we're not trying to
convert anyone…well, I'm not anyway. Just try to be
happy, alright?

RICH

Alright, thanks.

*(RICH leaves. CHRIS is still looking after him as he
leaves. AJ notices he's gone and stops rifling through
the wallet. He puts it behind his back as CHRIS turns
around.)*

CHRIS

Think he'll be alright?
*(He says this as he sits down at the table and finally
scoops on some cold Veal Parmigian.)*

AJ

Fine, just fine.
(Sits down.)

CHRIS

Well, I hope so. Things gotta turn up for him soon,
right?

AJ

Well, on the brighter side, it can't get much worse.
(From off-stage, we hear RICH scream)

RICH

Ah, shit! Now where's my wallet!
*(CHRIS slams his fork down on his plate and shoots a
hard look at AJ eating his food.)*

AJ
(With a full mouth.)

What?

END SCENE 1

SCENE 2—*The Chinese Restaurant. This scene is a long set,
where the entrance to the restaurant is far stage right, there are many
small tables in the middle, and a small card table and folding chairs
far stage left. Next to the table are two doors, one to the restroom and
one to the kitchen. There are many Asian artifacts all around, adding
to the Chinese atmosphere. AJ is wearing a suit but takes off his tie as
they walk in and he puts it in his inside pocket. CHRIS comes in
wearing baggy jogging pants and a sweatshirt. As they walk in by the*

"Please wait to be seated" sign, they are admiring their watches, which are very nice.

CHRIS
(Comes in the door looking at his watch on his wrist.)
I gotta tell ya, A, this time a year gets better all the time.

AJ
Uncle Mike has gone above and beyond this year, Chris. Rolex's! Jesus, I never thought I'd own one of these. He must be looking to make a killing on this game Saturday.

CHRIS
Remember the World Series last year, when he got us each those big screen TV's? I almost fainted.

AJ
When I think of how much you got hooked up when I got you this job...You owe me so big it's ridiculous. And then...
(The host, SIMON, comes up. He knows the both of them, and is friendly and cordial.)

SIMON
Ah, I see you got my message, Mr. Malone.
(Nods to AJ)
Mr. Mitchell.

CHRIS
Seems to me you'd like to place a wager on this Saturday's game, Simon. And you know how I love to do my business in person.

SIMON
Especially where food is involved, I'm sure. Don't worry, I know the drill. Table for two in smoking. Uh, right this way.
(As SIMON leads them through the restaurant, AJ and CHRIS look around at the Chinese décor.)

AJ

Simon, I gotta tell you I'm real impressed. Who decided on these new decorations? Whole new feel to the restaurant.

SIMON
(Uneasy)

Uh, the owner, Mr. Shattenstein, he came through about a week ago and made some changes, some small…some big.

CHRIS
(Just before they arrive at the table.)

Well, I gotta tell ya, if I didn't know any better I'd think I was in downtown Beijing…
(Fades as he approaches the table that SIMON brings them to. It is a card table with folding chairs with the bathroom door on one side and the kitchen doors on the other.)

What…what is this?

SIMON
(Sighing)

This…is the smoking section. This is one of the main changes Mr. Shattenstein made. It seems that people who do not smoke do not wish to be around those who do, and the non-smokers always outnumber the smokers so…

AJ

So that makes it okay to put us at Uncle Joe's card table in between the kitchen and the bathroom? Jesus, Simon, if we wanted this kind of atmosphere we'd eat in my parent's basement. This is the whole smoking section?

SIMON

Yes, this is it.

CHRIS

This is segregation!

SIMON

Please, I really wish you wouldn't say that word.

CHRIS

Afraid of bad public relations, eh?

SIMON

No, it just sounds too much like "immigration," and I don't need my whole cooking staff running out the back door. Fellas, I really am sorry about this, but…it's a supply/demand thing.

(He walks back to the kitchen door and swings it back, calling into it in Spanish.)

No, no. Es bueno. No es la migra.

(And he disappears into the kitchen.)

AJ

(Calling after SIMON)

Keep it up and it'll be a "boycott the restaurant" thing.

(They both look at the sorry excuse for a table that they have.)

CHRIS

Well, you want the kitchen, or the bathroom?

AJ

I'll take the bathroom. I'll chuck my butts in there as a sign of protest.

CHRIS

Who'd have guessed you were such an activist?

AJ

Man's gotta have principles.

(They sit down.)

I personally think they sat us here because of your current appearance.

CHRIS

Oh, would you get off that, please.

AJ

I can't believe you went to see Uncle Mike like that. He calls you in to give you this elegant and high-class gift…and you look like a bum.

(He lights a cigarette and hands one to Chris as well.)

CHRIS

Look, I told you what happened. I thought I could get in a workout before I was gonna meet Uncle Mike, but there was too much traffic on 95 for me to get changed in time.

AJ

What are you doing at the fitness club in the first place?

CHRIS

I'm signed up for a one year membership. I might as well use it from time to time.

AJ

Didn't I tell you not to sign anything unless I was present? Remember what happened the last time you joined a health club?

CHRIS

I thought we agreed not to mention the girl-on-girl shit again. Besides, this time they caught me at a moment of weakness. I wanted to get in shape and they offered me a good deal. So I joined.

AJ

40 bucks a month just to lift weights is not a good deal, Chris.

CHRIS

It's not just weights, smart guy. They've got top notch aerobic equipment, Olympic size swimming pool, basketball court…

AJ

(Interrupting)

Are you listening to yourself? You're spouting their propaganda like you've been brainwashed. Well, you can save the sales pitch alright. I ain't joinin' nothin'.

CHRIS

You laugh and you jest, but in the short time I've been a member, I feel that I've gotten bigger. And quite frankly I'm a little upset you haven't noticed.

(The waiter comes to the table. His name is FRED. He is a large black man dressed in authentic Chinese garb.)
AJ
That's just…
(Stops as he sees FRED. After a pause, AJ and CHRIS laugh uncontrollably.)
AJ
Fred, what is…?
(Laughing still)
…is this your outfit now?
FRED
Yeah, you like this? Part of the new changes around here. They decided to ditch the regular white shirt, black tie look that I had become so accustomed to, and to adopt this…
(Points out his outfit.)
…as a way to appear more authentic.
CHRIS
Well, I don't know about you fellas, but nothing screams "authenticity" like a six foot black man dressed like something out of the Ming dynasty. Is this a phase…something their trying out or do you think it'll be permanent?
FRED
I don't know, but it's getting really old real fast. Sure, it's not that bad at work, but I gotta walk five blocks lookin' like this.
AJ
That's a bummer, man, but as long as we're griping about current policy changes around here, take a look at our smoking section. It's the size of the bathroom.
FRED
Yeah, I kind of figured you guys wouldn't like it. But hey, on the brighter side, they were thinking of making the whole restaurant non-smoking, but I guess Simon

remembered you guys and insisted on at least one table. You guys should feel pretty special.

AJ

Special!? Fred, we're at a freakin' card table! This is the kind of table they set up for kids at Thanksgiving.

FRED

Alright, alright, point taken. Listen, in light of our respective grievances…How about I bring you guys a bottle of the good stuff? Simon's private reserve.

AJ

Private reserve? Man, I knew Simon's been holdin' out on us. The only wine he ever gives us on the house is from Kansas.

CHRIS

Although I have grown fond of a good Wichita '96.

FRED

Well, I'll get that as a backup. But as my first choice, let's see if we can get something foreign.

CHRIS

You ever been to Kansas? It's foreign enough for me.
(FRED leaves, into the kitchen.)

AJ

Can you believe this? This place too? So many places are doing away with the whole smoking section! It's ridiculous. Whatever happened to "separate but equal?"

CHRIS

I'm not sure the spirit of that phrase was meant to apply to our particular situation. Well, push comes to shove, I guess we'll just have to get used to going outside.

AJ

Going outside? What are we…animals? If we smoke do we not bleed?
(Fidgeting, stuttering.)

I…We…We should do…What can we do? We
have…We have to make a point here! I gotta do
something.

(He gets up.)
CHRIS
(CHRIS grabs AJ as he gets up.)
Please, no points here. Don't prove any points here.
Every time you use this place to make one of your
points, Simon has to pull me aside and ask me to calm
you down. And he does it in this way that makes me
feel like shit. So, if we could avoid that whole
conversation I would really appreciate it. Make your
point somewhere else. Just…Just sit down.

AJ
Would you relax, I'm a big boy; I can take
responsibility for my own actions. If Simon has a
problem with my actions, just send him to me.
*(He gets up and walks towards the part of the set with
the tables of non-smokers.)*
CHRIS
(Calling after AJ)
He won't talk to you. You scare him.
*(AJ then walks amongst the tables that are only dimly
lit, he talks to the people that are there but he is not
heard. The lights stay up on CHRIS.)*
CHRIS
(To the audience.)
He always has to make a point. Of course, I think a lot
of people do that now, though. Too many people have
become confident in their opinions…on
everything…and they feel the need to express that
opinion every chance they get. For example, take my
theories on music. I think popular songs in the hearts
of most people are widely misconstrued. The one I find
most people get wrong is Lesley Gore's song "Judy's
Turn to Cry." This was her sequel to her song "It's my
Party and…" well, we all know the rest. The premise

of the first song was easy. It's the narrator's birthday and at her party her boyfriend dumps her for her slutty friend, Judy…de de de…she's crying and everybody's sad. Now the sister song, "Judy's turn to cry," is supposed to be the song that makes everyone happy because said narrator gets her man back. That is the feeling most people come away with after this song, but I stipulate that they are merely scratching the surface of this twisted tale. Let's look at lyrics, shall we. The narrator uses the first verse to recap the situation from her first song, but the title and therefore the chorus revolves around how she plans to get Johnny back, which seems to me a ridiculous concept in the first place, cause why would she want to get back with the kind of prick that would leave her for one of her friends at her own birthday party. But wait! That's not even the worst part! The plan that the narrator has for reclaiming her man is to make Johnny jealous, so at another party she goes and kisses some other guy, let's call him Carl, just for laughs. This moment of passion with Carl infuriates Johnny, who has no right to be furious, mind you, so he goes and punches out Carl, thus reaffirming his love for the narrator, so she's real happy and now it's "Judy's Turn to Cry." So everything's back the way it was, and everyone's happy, right? Hello! What everyone seems to forget here, is that a perfectly innocent bystander has been physically assaulted and publicly humiliated, all because of one bitch's selfish needs. A victim of the narrator's plan, Carl just thought he was getting lucky at a party. Now, since this was all part of an elaborate plan, the narrator more than likely came on to him, more than likely something that doesn't happen to him very often. He plays along…starts making out with her, actually feeling good about himself, and what does he get…A punch in the face!! And why? So some stupid chic could get back with a boyfriend that treats

105

her like shit. What people forget is that these two songs
are actually part of a trilogy. The slightly less popular
third part was entitled, "It's my turn to cry again
because Johnny knocked me up at 16 and now he beats
me." Sure, it's depressing, but it's got a beat and you
can dance to it.

*(AJ comes back to the table with 3 other people from
the restaurant. Two guys and a woman. As he
introduces them, he hands each of them a cigarette
from his pack.)*

CHRIS

Alright, okay…now who are these people?

AJ

Chris, I would like you to meet Heather, Todd and
Mark…

(Searching)

…Marcus.

*(As each of them put the cigarettes in their mouth, AJ
goes around lighting them.)*

They are honest, hardworking people who have a
particular habit which they are being forced to hide for
one reason or another, so I took it upon myself to
rescue them from their prison in non-smoking to our
sanctuary shores.

CHRIS

What's the point, exactly?

AJ

I'm getting there. I'm getting there. You see, the
smoking sections of all these different places have
been cut down or totally done away with because
people think that nobody smokes anymore. But the fact
is, smokers have been forced by other people in their
lives to hide their habit and/or seek other outlets for
their fixation.

(Gets a puzzled look on his face.)

Hey, none of you guys are on the patch, are you?

MARCUS & TODD

No.

HEATHER

No, but my husband's got me on the nicotine gum.

CHRIS

I heard about that stuff, what's the deal with that anyway?

HEATHER

It cuts down the cravings by slowly satisfying the nicotine my system needs and also makes me do something with my mouth. The oral fixation is another theory of why we smoke. Sounds kind of Freudian.

AJ

Let me try one. Let's see what this stuff is all about.

HEATHER

Sure.

(She pulls out a pack which looks a cough drop container.)

AJ

It comes looking like that? This must be some strong stuff. It looks all medical and shit.

(He pops one of the pieces and chews it for a while. Everyone just watches him as they smoke.)

MARCUS

Well, what do you think?

AJ

(Puzzled look on his face.)

It's kind of…it has no taste. I am experiencing nothing.

(He chews some more, as if he's trying hard to get something out of the gum. He then looks down at his cigarette in his hand, takes a long drag, then gets a big smile.)

Now that's where it's at! Whoa! See that's the trick, fellas…and lady…the gum itself is kind of boring, but take a long drag while chewing it and Hellzapoppin'! This stuff should be jumpin' off the shelves.

CHRIS

Once again you have astounded us all.
(Marcus and Todd start putting out their cigarettes though they have only smoked like half of them.)

AJ

Hey, hey, what are you doing? You hardly even smoked half that thing.

MARCUS

Sorry, man, but when you came around inviting people to smoke, I told my wife I thought you were crazy. I just told her I came back to use the bathroom.

AJ

What? Et tu, Todd?

TODD

Sorry AJ, as far as my wife knows, I haven't had a smoke in three months.
(CHRIS reaches in his pocket and pulls out some banaka spray and tosses it to TODD.)

TODD

Ah, man, you're a life saver.
(He sprays the banaka in his mouth and on his clothes. Then tosses it to Marcus.)

MARCUS

Thanks.
(He uses the spray then hands it to CHRIS.)

AJ

You mean you didn't even say why you came back here? Then how will they know...How can we accomplish anything if you didn't even say you came back to smoke?
(He sits back down defeated.)
I guess smoking sections have no chance of salvation.

HEATHER

Well, who can blame 'em? Nobody wants to be around this stuff while they eat.
(She puffs out her cigarette and puts it out as she leaves.)

108

AJ

Typical bitch. Big fuckin' surprise.

CHRIS

Cheer up, buckaroo. We'll get 'em next time.

(FRED comes out from the kitchen with a bottle of wine and two glasses.)

FRED

(He says these lines as he is pouring the wine for the guys.)

Sorry for the delay, fellas, but according to Simon you managed to keep yourselves busy. By the way, Mr. Malone, Simon said he wanted to talk to you before you leave.

CHRIS

(To AJ)

What did I tell you?

(To FRED)

How did he sound? Did he sound mad?

AJ

Listen to yourself…are you even listening…

CHRIS

(To FRED)

Hey, Fred, let me ask you something. You go to a gym or anything? You know, you lift or anything like that?

FRED

Yeah, I try to get to the gym about twice a week. Man's gotta work hard to feel tough when he has to wear an outfit like this five times a week. Got a membership at a place down on Meridian. Why? You thinking of joining or something?

AJ

No, Mr. Universe here already signed a year contract at some other place. Down on Harrison, right?

CHRIS

(Dismissing AJ)

About how much you bench, if you don't mind my asking?

FRED

Nah, I don't mind. I bench around 240-250. How about you?

CHRIS

Hey, thanks for the wine.
(Looks at the bottle)
Looks pretty good. Old and French, that's really all you need. I think we're just gonna split an order of Sesame Chicken and a large bowl of steamed rice.

FRED
(Surprised but not really by the change of subject.)
Okay…Uh…no soup?

AJ
(To CHRIS.)

Yeah, no soup?

CHRIS

Get soup if you want. I'm fine, thanks.

AJ

I'll take a bowl of egg drop, please. Thanks, Fred. Oh, and in addition to the steamed rice could I get a bowl of fried rice on the side. Variety is the spice of life.

FRED

That's what I told my first wife when she caught me with a perfume girl from Macy's. I'll be right out with that soup, and I'll tell the cooks to get on that Sesame Chicken.

(He leaves.)
CHRIS

Thanks, Fred.
(Now just to AJ)
See, that's the problem I have with the whole gym experience.

AJ

I can't believe you only have one problem.

CHRIS

When I go in, I have a very basic routine, nothing too strenuous or anything, just a few sets of bench and arm exercises, because those are the only things I really care about. But at the same time, even in the limited time that I'm in there, I don't feel comfortable enough with the people...perfect strangers...to ask anyone to spot me. And because I'm so weak, I can only lift like 100-120 pounds, while everyone around me is doing 200's. I just feel like they're all looking down at me, or even worse, I think when I leave they get together and make jokes about me. I'd try to go higher in weight but then I'm afraid I wouldn't be able to lift that off my chest and I'll be crushed by the weight...Which would be the preferred ending to the situation, because I'd rather die at one of those places then ask someone to help lift the weights off me.

                    AJ
So, what you're saying is, you pay 46 dollars a month to go to a place that humiliates you and may eventually kill you?

                  CHRIS
Yes.

                    AJ
You know, the funny thing is, it was your own insecurities that led you there in the first place, and now it's those same insecurities that are making the place practically unbearable.

                  CHRIS
You gonna suggest a solution anytime soon, or just keep pointing out elements of the problem?

                    AJ
Jesus, Chris, just look at the people that are at the gym with you. The way I see it, most of them are there for one of three reasons.
            (He uses his fingers to count them out.)
One, they're either there only to meet young attractive members of the opposite sex, so they act like adolescents trying to impress one another. Two, they got into a habit of working out for a high school sport

and are still holding fast to the delusion that they can recapture their glory days. This is ridiculous in itself, because I don't care what your coach may have told you, at 30, you ain't makin' varsity. Or three, they are just as insecure as you are and they look forward to seeing guys in there that lift less than them because for those brief moments that you're in there, they feel like they're better than someone else. It's a momentary vacation from the pathetic shambles that their lives have become.

CHRIS

So your solution is…?

AJ

Keep going' until somebody comes in who lifts less than even you, and join the others in making fun of him.

CHRIS

Sounds like a plan.

(FRED comes back on with a bowl of soup and a soup spoon for AJ.)

FRED

Here ya go, one bowl of egg drop, and that sesame chicken should be out in a second.

AJ

Thanks, Fred.

(SIMON comes out and whispers something in CHRIS' ear. CHRIS then pulls out a small book and writes something in it. SIMON then gets up to leave but looks at AJ then leans in and talks to CHRIS again. Then gives him a stern look and leaves.)

AJ

Why are my ears burning?

CHRIS

Take a guess.

(FRED sees his small book on the table. He picks it up.)

FRED

Big game this Saturday, eh? How much money will
change hands based on these numbers in here?

AJ

That's the beauty of the business. No matter how much
money changes hands, we always end up on top.

FRED

You guys ever have any trouble collecting...you
know...people ever hold out on you?

CHRIS

Sometimes, but that's one of the benefits of workin'
for somebody like Uncle Mike. God knows AJ and I
don't exactly inspire the kind of feelings necessary for
people to hand over their hard earned cash. But Uncle
Mike's respected, and in some cases feared, by most
everyone in the gambling community, and his
influence and contacts make it easy to collect, even on
the most reluctant client.

FRED

And what about people not so well acquainted with the
gambling community?

AJ

We have to be very selective with those types. Some
people...we just won't accept their bets if we don't
trust 'em. And with big events like the game this
Saturday, the freaks come out of the woodwork. Our
judgement has to be pretty sharp.

CHRIS

Well, sometimes the decision is pretty easy. Like, just
today,
(To AJ real quick)
I was gonna tell you about this later...
(Now back to FRED)
...this woman calls my cell...got it from another
client...and asks if she put some money down on
Saturday's game. I can't just put somebody down...
(Holding up book)

113

...without knowing who they are, where they work...basic characteristics. It's kind of like applying for a loan.

CHRIS... wait

AJ
That's exactly what it's like.

CHRIS
So, I meet this chick at Starbucks for a cup of the hard stuff, and she shows me the forms of ID and all that, and then we get into what she does. She works as an assistant to the Vice President in charge of marketing for the Orlando Magic.

FRED
Hey, impressive!

CHRIS
That's not the best part. It's a real Cinderella story with this girl. Turns out she used to be on the Magic's dance team. You know, the half-time dancers, and she did that to work her way to a degree in business. Once she had that, she moved right into the marketing office, no problem. You know, because she had the contacts.

AJ
I love the dance teams. They're kind of like the cheerleaders who were the bad girls in high school. Their outfits are sexier, their moves are sexier, and they could give two shits about whether the team wins, so they ain't gotta do any of that Rah Rah bullshit that the cheerleaders gotta do. They're less annoying than cheerleaders...and dirtier.

FRED
So this girl cleared, right?

CHRIS
Yeah, and this girl's a real gem. She's pickin' Florida over FSU because she used to date one of the assistants for Florida State. She dropped a nickel on a bet against the favorites out of spite. That's gonna be a fun collection to make. And let me tell you, Fred, this girl was something else. Great body, Barbie-like, you

know, with the good stuff up top and the thin
waist…and legs, whoa, legs that took the long way
down to the floor.

                    AJ
What's her name?

                  CHRIS
Angela, you know like "Who's The Boss?"
                (Tony Danza voice.)
Hey Angela, it's Tony Danza over here.

                    AJ
Man, he should have quit after "Taxi." She got a last
name?

                  CHRIS
Angela Demarcos.

                    AJ
Jesus, $500 on the Gators because of an ex-boyfriend.
After you collect from her, we ought to head down to
Florida State, find that guy and buy him dinner.

                  CHRIS
You're on; it's been a while since I've been down to
FSU. Oh, AJ, and you would have loved to hear this
girl talk about the guy. The bitterness in this girls
voice…it could shatter glass. This fella hurt her…hurt
her bad. Oh, it's gonna be fun collecting on this one.

                    AJ
Say, Fred, where's Meredith? She not workin' tonight?

                  FRED
She tries to cut down her hours now. She just waits till
later in the evenings, you know, when most dates
occur. She should be out shortly, though. I saw her
prepping her basket in back. I'll send her to you guys
first…you're pretty easy to find.
            (He leaves into the kitchen.)
                    AJ
Very funny.
    *(He flicks a cigarette butt into the bathroom. Then he
          looks around the restaurant.)*

Well, what do you say, Chris? You see any takers here tonight? Pickings seem pretty slim, looks like a married crowd...Oh, wait a minute...
(Pointing at a couple towards the back, as the lights come up on a young teenage couple.)
...young couple in the back could be the subjects for tonight.

CHRIS
(Sees them as the lights come up on the couple.)
Yeah, good eye. Looks like a first date...maybe second.
(MEREDITH comes from the kitchen. She is an older woman carrying a basket full of carnations.)
MEREDITH
Hey, boys! Fred said you were here tonight. So, how you likin' your new accommodations?

CHRIS
Meredith, please don't get him started. So, how's business?
(Notices the flowers.)
Hey, goin' with carnations now, eh?

MEREDITH
Yeah, the guy I use raised the prices on his roses, so I gotta downgrade a bit.

AJ
Kept the price the same, though, I see.

MEREDITH
Hey, what they don't know...

CHRIS
And how's Roger? The dry cleaning business still as lucrative and glamorous as everyone says?

MEREDITH
Ugh, I wish he would just sell the store and be done with it. He sweats off ten pounds a day in that place, I swear to God. But I guess the business people of the world need pressed suits. Just like the couples of the world need flowers.

AJ
Well, I think you've got your work cut out for you tonight, darling. We don't see much in the way of buyers this evening.

CHRIS
Although this couple towards the back here looks most promising.

MEREDITH
(Eyes the couple, who are just talking.)
Could go either way. It's so hard to tell these days. Where's your money, AJ?

AJ
(Taking out his wallet. Putting a twenty on the table.)
I'm gonna go with no sale. Not a comment on your sales technique, mind you, Meredith, I know you're the best. But I think guys are getting wise to the flowers scam…not falling for it as easy as most in the past.

CHRIS
Alright…
(Puts his money on the table.)
…I say he gets her one.
(Touching MEREDITH's face.)
Who could say no to this face? Besides, I think there are a few more chumps left in the world.

AJ
Well, so do I, but I guess I figure most of them are scattered in various weight rooms around the country.

CHRIS
Easy, comrade.

AJ
Alright, flower lady. Do your worst.

CHRIS
Let's see what this kid is made of.
(MEREDITH walks over to the young couple who can be seen and not heard, she talks to them for a while but she cannot be heard either. The boys talk while she is selling.)

117

                    AJ
God, I use to hate dating.
                  CHRIS
No you didn't. Not at the beginning. People don't start
to hate the scene until they've been in it for a while.
Then they loathe it. At the beginning, it's some new
and bold adventure, you felt like Magellan on some
daring voyage of exploration.
                    AJ
What is it with you and Magellan? If you're gonna
pick an explorer, pick a conquistador. Pick someone
who would kill the natives with impunity.
                  CHRIS
        (Looking at the couple. In the distance, the kid is
                reaching for his wallet.)
Oh, you're not gonna be happy with this.
                    AJ
              (Looking as well.)
No, no! Why is he getting out his wallet?
                  CHRIS
Well, when you think about it...
        (CHRIS takes the money off the table.)
...there could only be one reason.
          (Puts the twenties in his wallet.)
                    AJ
I don't believe this! He's not buying one, he's buying
her two of those frickin' carnations.
                  CHRIS
What?
                    AJ
Yeah, look.
                  CHRIS
Oh, man, that kid wants it bad.
(AJ grabs his wine glass and heads towards the young
couple. CHRIS is still putting his wallet away in his
pocket so he does not have time to grab him, but he
calls after him as he goes.)

                    118

CHRIS

AJ! AJ, don't...
(But AJ is at the table already.)

AJ
(To the kid.)

What the hell are you doing?
*(CHRIS has gotten up and he pulls AJ back to the
smoking section while the kids are left sitting with
puzzled looks on their faces.)*

CHRIS

I'm not gonna let you do it this time, AJ! I'm not
gonna let it happen. You may have shit in a lot of
people's soup over the years, and I sat and watched,
hell I even enjoy most of 'em, but this is a kid on a
date with a girl, maybe even his first date, and I
remember how those were, cause I've been on a lot of
'em. And believe me, this kids got enough to worry
about right now. All that shit...how's my hair, do my
shoes match my belt, am I being too complimentary,
am I not complementing enough...Jesus, don't you
remember that? And the last thing I would have
wanted, the last thing I would wish to inflict on
anybody in that situation, is to have guys like us, two
bitter, insensitive assholes, come into the picture and
add that much more anxiety and tension. I won't let
you do it! Let's just sit down at our table in our little
smoking section, and leave the outside world alone,
just for once, eh? Just for laughs!

AJ

Chris, I think you're old enough now to know this. The
reason we were so nervous about all those things when
we were first dating...is because we are meek.

CHRIS

We're meek?

AJ

Yep, when we first got into dating we were not
assertive enough with the women we dated. And you

119

know how women talk, so we got reputations as guys that women could walk all over and it continued from there and that led to our feelings of inadequacy, which led to our current state of bitterness. Now this kid is on the road to that inadequacy, I saw it...plain as day...I saw it the second he bought those flowers. We have the chance to save him. Through the benefit of our experience, we can save him from the bitterness and ineptitude that we felt and still feel today.

CHRIS

(Pause, thinking.)

So you actually have good intentions here?

AJ

I always have good intentions. Don't make me out to be some kind of ogre, Chris, I just don't mask my message with all the frilly bullshit that people want to hear. I'm giving lessons on life, and life is hard. You shouldn't have to sugar coat it.

CHRIS

I think I really am meek. I'm letting you talk me into this.

AJ

Just relax and let me do all the talking...And if the girl tries to chime in or anything, you know, starts mouthin' off, I give you permission to slap her around a little bit.

(AJ walks back over to the kids table, he stands as he talks to the kids. CHRIS pulls his folding chair over from his table and sits down in it near their table, simply a bystander.)

AJ

(To the kid, who is called JAMES.)

I'm sorry for my outburst just then. I realize it requires an explanation. I just...My friend and I saw you buying flowers for your, your lovely date here and I was just a little shocked.

JAMES

Shocked, sir? Why is it shocking for a guy to buy a flower for his date?

AJ

Not just one, not one, you bought two. If you'd have only bought one, my soup wouldn't be getting cold now. You bought two flowers for...

(Snapping his fingers trying to get the girl's name, which is TIFFANY.)

TIFFANY

(Blankly.)

Tiffany.

AJ

Thank you. You bought two flowers for Tiff here. Let's stick to the facts, okay?

JAMES

Alright, so I bought her two flowers.

AJ

The flowers were 7 bucks a piece, kid. Don't you see how you got played? Can't you see how your position as the guy on a date has been exploited?

(Before AJ has a chance to finish his point, JAMES has gotten up out of his chair, said a quiet "Excuse me" to TIFFANY, and moved over to the smoking section. AJ just looks at him for a while, but then JAMES motions him over to talk. CHRIS is left alone with TIFFANY.)

CHRIS

So, Tiffany...'bout how much you bench?

(Now the conversation between AJ and JAMES is focused upon, back in the smoking section.)

JAMES

Look, sir, I'm not really sure what it is you're trying to prove here, but in the brief moments we have together before I let you get back to your dinner here...

(Notices the table.)

Hey, is this a card table? Anyway, let me tell you a little bit about myself. I am a senior in high school, and

121

over these last four years, my social calendar hasn't
been terribly packed. I don't play any sports. I'm not in
any clubs. My family is not rich, and I drive a Dodge
Stratus…and I'm not sure how it was for you in high
school, but women usually don't flock to a man
because his car gets 25 a gallon in the city. Now, that
girl there…she's a cheerleader. A cheerleader! And
how I got a date with her at all is a matter of dumb
luck alone. This girl…This is a girl whose name has
found its way onto every bathroom stall at my school.
And sir, it's a very large school. Alright, you caught
me! I bought her those flowers to try to impress her.
It's the same reason I took her to this restaurant. Hell, I
hate Chinese food! But there is a consensus view as to
how high school life is supposed to go, and I am
lacking in one very important aspect of that view. Now
this girl has a reputation for being very good at that
particular aspect, and to try to get even an inch closer
to experiencing her expertise in this field I'd buy her
an entire frickin' garden if she asked for one, let alone
two lousy overpriced carnations.
MEREDITH
(From a little further off to stage left.)
Hey!
JAMES
And yet, after buying those flowers, instead of
experiencing any display of gratitude from her, I'm
talking to you, a complete stranger, in this shoebox of
a smoking section. What's wrong with this picture?
AJ
Really, you get twenty-five a gallon in the city?
JAMES
Am I on some hidden video thing?
(TIFFANY has a cell phone ring in her coat pocket.
She answers it and talks on it and is not heard. AJ
notices her on the cell phone, CHRIS just shrugs his
shoulders in an "I don't know" motion.)

122

AJ

Look, kid, throw some money on the table and just get the hell out, as fast as you can. Trust me.

JAMES

Trust you? Who are you?

AJ

Listen, here's what's gonna happen. You're treatin' this girl great tonight. She's at a classy restaurant, you got her flowers, you've probably complemented her eight billion times already...but the only display of gratitude you're gonna get from her is a hug at best. And then tomorrow, she's gonna tell all her friends about tonight, and they'll giggle and laugh in their stupid girl way, and then that night she'll go out and bang the shit out of the offensive line after they buy her a hamburger.

JAMES
(Offended.)

She told me that story was just a rumor.

(AJ just points at him. There is a pause as JAMES sits in the chair that is left.)

If what you're saying is true, then you're telling me I can't score with a girl who's been described as easier than a kindergarten jigsaw puzzle. You wouldn't happen to be a motivational speaker, by any chance, would you?

(TIFFANY leaves CHRIS at the table and goes to JAMES and AJ.)

TIFFANY

Um, I'm not sure what this is all about, but Steph just called and there's apparently a little get-together at her place right now. It's just a few girls from the squad and the basketball team playing drinking games.

JAMES

That sounds good, I was actually getting pretty tired of this place anyway.

TIFFANY

Uh, James, I pleaded and pleaded, but apparently some
of the basketball players had a problem with the
equipment manager being at a player's party.

AJ

And you said you didn't play any sports.

TIFFANY

I am sorry the night had to end like this, but I will
make it up to you, I promise.

(Puts on her jacket.)

And I do thank you for dinner. Oh, and one last thing.
Can I use your car to get to Steph's place? I have to
pick up a few of the players on the way. I'm sure one
of your friends here can give you a ride home.

*(AJ and CHRIS run their hands down their faces.
JAMES just hands over the keys like he doesn't know
what's going on.)*

JAMES

Alright.

(Pause.)

Drive safe.

TIFFANY

Oh, you're a sweetheart. I'll tell you all about the
party. Goodbye.

(Walks off-stage.)
*(When she has left the stage, JAMES finally has a
grasp of what he has done and who is watching.)*

JAMES

*(Calling after TIFFANY but she is gone and he knows
it. He calls after her in a deep Eddie Murphy voice.)*
But there better be gas in that car when I get it back.
*(JAMES sits down at the card table. Very down in the
dumps.)*

JAMES

I told myself I wouldn't let that happen again...Not
after the last time.

Act Like A Man
A Collection of Plays

*(AJ and CHRIS come back to their table, they both
bring a chair back to sit in.)*

AJ
(Offering a cigarette.)

You smoke, kid.

JAMES
(Waving it off.)

Nah. And it's James, by the way, you can stop calling
me "kid."

CHRIS

Not to appear nosier than I'm sure we already do, but I
was stuck with Blondie over there so I don't know the
whole story.

JAMES

Be happy, you spent more time with her than I did.

AJ
(To CHRIS)

Okay, here's the situation. Jimmy here isn't exactly
Joe Cool at school. He's a senior, about to graduate but
he doesn't feel he is as far along, sexually, as the
typical garden-variety senior.

JAMES

Okay, this is officially the worst I have ever felt in my
life.

AJ
(Continuing.)

He's not class president, drives a family car, and he
doesn't play a sport, although he's apparently the
equipment manager for the basketball team.

CHRIS

He's the water boy?

JAMES

Equipment manager, alright! Do not simplify my title!
A water boy just gets water! And I am not a towel boy
either...they just get towels. An equipment manager...

AJ
(Interrupting.)

125

Gets both water and towels. Anyway, Tiffany, the young lady who made a most abrupt and shamefully early exit, is apparently the Great White Hope for young Mr. James. She's a cheerleader at the school and in her short time there she has managed to acquire quite the reputation.

CHRIS

Details, I need details.

(AJ gestures to JAMES.)

JAMES

At a party once, one I was invited to…I guess she was really drunk or she might have done it on a dare…I actually saw her suck-start a vacuum cleaner.

(CHRIS and AJ are stunned and impressed.)

CHRIS & AJ

(Australian)

Crikey!

JAMES

I guess I'll just have to hold on to that memory for a while. Or ask the basketball players for a detailed account.

(He drinks the wine straight from the guys' bottle.)

Hey, not bad.

(Looking at the bottle.)

Old and French.

AJ

So, to recap, James is not gonna win any popularity contests any time soon at school, and he wants to pop a girl before he graduates. That about right?

JAMES

In a nutshell. Very elegantly put as well.

CHRIS

Not exactly known for tact, is he? How pressing is this graduation deadline, anyway? You gonna join the priesthood if you fail, or is it less extreme?

JAMES

I know I shouldn't make such a big deal about it, and I
know what it looks like, but I am not just another
horny teen-age kid...

AJ

Excuse me? Hey, if it looks like a duck, and sounds
like a duck...

JAMES

Alright! So I am just another horny teen-age kid! But I
am also grounded in reality, okay? I listened to all the
lectures. I know sex is an important step in maturity, I
know that ideally it should take place between two
people in love, I know that it's something you don't go
into lightly...and blah blah blah.

(Another drink.)

CHRIS

You don't seem to buy it.

JAMES

That's relationship sex they're talking about. And, to
be as tactful as your friend here, I just wanna get
boned. I'll have time enough for relationship stuff
when I get older and I know what I'm looking for.
Right now, I'm not ready to deal with all the emotional
baggage that comes with relationship sex. I'm just a
kid. I still rush home after school to watch cartoons,
for Christ's sake.

AJ

Not that Pokemon stuff, right? I swear to God the
Japanese are trying to brainwash us with that shit. I
mean, really, what the hell is that?

JAMES

(Ignoring him)

And the people at school, the guys that have steady
girlfriends and have taken that step and had sex with
their girls...You should see 'em. They walk on
eggshells with everything they say, so worried as to
what the woman will think of it. Some just plain give

up and ask their woman what to say. Their big problem
is, after the sex, the woman is still there…always…and
she wants to talk about it. The only people the guy
wants to talk about it with is the other guys, because he
can lie his ass off to them.
(Imitating a guy talking about sex.)
"Oh, I did this, and she screamed that and we were
almost arrested for doing this…" The chicks want to
talk about inner feelings and intimacy. And guys are
willing to gnaw their own arms off to get away from
talkin' about shit like that.

CHRIS

All valid points.

JAMES

Right now, I'm so sexually frustrated, I can't even
spell words like relationship or commitment or
intimacy. I'm just looking for…

AJ

Sport sex.

JAMES
(Points at him.)
Yeah, "sport sex." It's even got a cool name. I don't
want to have one of those experiences that people
could look at and say, "Ahhh, the act of love…Tra La
La." You know all rose petals and pretty candles and
shit. I want the kind of experience that scares people. I
want to be sore the next day. I want the kind of first
time that I can look back on and guys will just step
back and applaud.
(Pause.)
I wanna break shit.
(CHRIS and AJ just stand back stunned.)
CHRIS
All this sentimentality is making me weepy.

AJ
You ever thought of goin' to a pro. Sometimes they
give you a discount if you let them break shit.

128

JAMES

Get outta here.

AJ

No, I'm serious. If you get a good one, you don't have to worry about disease or pregnancy, all that shit that takes the initial pleasure out of your first time. I'm telling you, most of these women take better care of their bodies than Olympic athletes.

CHRIS

Except after their events, instead of Gatorade they reach for a cigarette.

(JAMES still wrenches at the thought of a hooker.)

AJ

And maybe I have only known you a short while, but you can't be objecting on religious grounds. I think your comment about breaking shit pretty much knocked you out of the priesthood. And I don't get how religious people can be down on the oldest profession anyway. Mary Magdelan was one of the biggest names in the Bible, she was a hooker, and she was supposedly Jesus' girlfriend. You can't tell me he didn't have to pay for it once in a while.

CHRIS

They reserve special places in hell for people who say that.

JAMES

It's not religious. I only make it to church three times a year, and in my daily routine, I could give two shits what Jesus would do. There is just something very desperate and very wrong about paying for sex…especially your first time.

AJ

Jesus Christ! What do you think you were just doing?

CHRIS

Alright, that's three references to the son of God in a row. I'm not overly religious either, but last time I checked, God was still pretty keen on smiting.

129

                                 AJ
You were out on a date with this girl, this Tiff girl,
trying to get her into bed, or into car or whatever…and
what did you have to do? You had to take her to
dinner, which is about 15 per person. A movie after
dinner would have put you out 8 bucks a piece, I
believe that is the current level of movie theater
extortion, and popcorn and soda another 10. That puts
the garden variety date at…what?
                              CHRIS
$56 dollars.

                                 AJ
Lest we forget the 10 extra dollars you spent on two
carnations. $66 dollars. If you didn't get it done on one
date, you go for two and you're up to 130. And the
whole time you have to say the right things, wear the
right clothes, act the right way in order to get into her
pants, even pants as easily accessible as young
Tiffany's.
                              JAMES
And the alternate route…
                                 AJ
You make a simple phone call, and a lovely woman
comes to you. No dinner beforehand. No futile,
monotonous conversation. No flowers. Just…
                              CHRIS
Breakin' shit.
                                 AJ
Exactly.
        (Reaches for his wallet, pulls out a card.)
Here's a suggestion. Tina Koslowsky. Very
respectable, caters to all needs, accepts all major credit
cards.
            (He hands the card to JAMES.)
She still owes me fifty on a Marlin game from this
summer. Hell, have her knock it off your tab.

CHRIS

She's got her own business card?

(Grabs it from JAMES)

Ah, "entertainment coordinator," very tactful. And you gotta respect the fact that she uses her real name. Most hookers change it for dramatic effect, you know, like Amber Waves or...Breasts Aplenty.

JAMES

Yeah, no one would change their name to Koslowsky.

AJ

That's what I'm saying, she's a professio...Breasts Aplenty?! That's the name you come up with? Breasts Aplenty?

CHRIS

Sorry, all the good names were taken by Bond girls. I was pressed for time.

JAMES

Look, I can appreciate...actually I really can't appreciate anything you're doing here, but the fact is we are discussing my first sexual experience here. And while I'm sure...

(Picks up the card)

...Ms. Koslowsky is a genius in her field, I don't want to reminisce on my passage into manhood and say I got it as a blue light special off a stranger. Now...

(Puts the card back down on the table.)

...if you'll excuse me.

(He walks back to his table and puts money on it.)

While I will cherish the memories of this conversation...

(To CHRIS.)

...especially Breasts Aplenty...thanks to a girl probably getting the better part of our teams starting center right about now, I have a bus to catch.

(He puts on a jacket, high school kids jacket, but not a letter jacket. Starts to walk off, then stops.)

You know, I always knew I was behind the curve, but that's always how I thought of myself…just behind the curve. I never felt pathetic until I met you two.
(He walks off.)
CHRIS
Boy, does that take me back.
AJ
Was that an attempt to inflict guilt? All we've done since we met that kid is try to help him. Where's the gratitude?
CHRIS
I don't know. That kid's shoes are remarkably similar to the one's I was in at his age…
(Picks up the card.)
And if you handed me a gem like this back then, I'd have sold my body to science for a night with her. Maybe there's something to be said for self-restraint.
(JAMES walks back on stage and grabs the card out of CHRIS's hand, then walks back off without a word.)
AJ
(Calling after him.)
Don't forget the AJ discounted fee.
(Back to CHRIS after a pause.)
Life's too short for self-restraint.
CHRIS
Well, if nothing else, in a few years our little group may have a third. Hey, like the Supremes.
AJ
If so, then I'm calling it right now…I get to be Diana Ross.
CHRIS
Damn!

END SCENE 2
END ACT ONE
CURTAIN

Act Two

SCENE 1—*The All-Night Diner. This is a diner like Denny's. There is a counter at the front with scattered tables about the room, with an ashtray on every table. There is a cook behind the counter and a waitress wearing an apron cleaning off one of the tables. There are two separate groups of kids, around age 16, with about 3 kids in each group. There is a table of two women at the side, and a man sitting at the counter.*
(As she speaks, the waitress, AMY, is wiping tables and refilling napkin dispensers.)
AMY
(To audience.)
Behold, the sleazy diner. The last bit of sanctuary for the dedicated smoker. A completely non-smoke free environment. The sections here include filtered and un-filtered. It's what heaven would be like if God's name was Philip Morris. Open 24 hours a day, 7 days a week…to all types of characters. We have no dress code, no maitre de.
(The cook laughs.)
You don't come here on a date, you don't come here with your boss for a power lunch, and at this time of night, it's just me and Archie there so you definitely don't come here for good service. You come here in the middle of the night to hang out with your friends, or when you just can't sleep. When you get off the late shift at whatever job you have and you just want to be around people. And to smoke. And when you do come here…from wherever…you're never trying to impress nobody, because…look around…who here would you want to impress? You come to these places to be real, at a time of night when real is all you can be.
(She lights a cigarette.)

133

So keep all open flames away from Archie's hair, and don't complain about the ashes in the food...The price of being real.

(AJ and CHRIS come in the front. AJ is wearing a long black coat over a sweatshirt and jeans. CHRIS is wearing a football jersey over running pants. He is going through his little book with a pen. CHRIS looks up as he walks towards the counter, then sees AMY.)

CHRIS

Amy, how are you? How's the week been?

AMY

Slow, as usual.

(She kisses him on the cheek.)

But getting better.

(Smile.)

Hey, AJ.

AJ

Evenin', Amy. Any takers tonight?

AMY

In the corner there. Some of 'em been waitin' for ya.

CHRIS

Say, how did Jaime do on his Biology test this week, anyway? It was Wednesday, right?

AMY

Yeah. He stayed up all night Tuesday puttin' those Biology facts into one of those big calculators, you know.

AJ

Many a class has been passed due to that very technique.

AMY

Maybe too many. Jaime's Biology teacher didn't feel there was any need for a calculator so he took it before the test.

CHRIS

So he did bad?

CENTER>AMY

No. As a backup plan he left his Biology book in the nearest bathroom. He just kept goin' there every five minutes lookin' up stuff.

AJ

And the teacher didn't get suspicious?

AMY

On the third trip, he induced vomiting.

CHRIS

Nice.

AMY

Yep, that's my boy. Take a seat, fellas. I'll get Archie on your food in a second.

CHRIS

Thanks.

(They go to a table STAGE LEFT and CHRIS sits down. AJ remains standing and tells CHRIS.)

AJ

Be right back.

(AJ walks over to the kids.)

What's happening, tikes? Heard you were looking for me.

(The kids walk over to AJ. They all start talking in a jumbled collection. The gist concerns cigarettes.)

Now, easy everyone, let's not get out of hand here.

(He opens his jacket and reveals the many packs of cigarettes he has in his jacket.)

Now, we got Marlboros and Camels over here on the right and Winston's and Salem's over on the left. The Menthols are towards the bottom and everything is filtered. Just my way of saying I care.

(The kids all grab various packs from his jacket, then start handing him money.)

Kids, Christmas is coming early this year. I'm waving my usual ten dollar fee. Just remember, if you have younger brothers or sisters…share, alright?

(He hands them books of matches.)

Enjoy.
(AJ walks back to his table, CHRIS is sitting down going through his book.)
CHRIS
(Not looking up.)
Working up quite a reputation, aren't ya?
AJ
God, I would make a great father.
CHRIS
No, I think you're tailor-made to be somebody's weird uncle.

AJ
Say what you will, but the kids, C, they are the future. If you want policy changes made in regards to the future of smoking, we need to get as many of these kids smoking as possible. And not that social smoking bullshit, either. I want them to need at least 4 a day, and shake at night when they only have three.
CHRIS
I can see you at the Pearly Gates right now, with a little card that reads: Go directly to hell, do not pass go do not collect 200 dollars. And have you looked at these kids, AJ? If this is the future we got bigger things to worry about than smoking.

AJ
God, Chris, why not complete the ensemble and wear a black robe and carry a gavel. These kids will be fine. There a smart bunch...sort of. Besides, sixteen is nothing. These kids can become anything in the next 5...10 years. That's why you gotta get 'em on the way up, before they know better. And it'd be easier for them if all these friggin' places around weren't so strict on their "We ID" policies. You know even I got checked at the Shell station two nights ago? My wallet was in the car so I had to walk all the way back out and get it, then back inside. I asked to speak with the manager, but...

CHRIS

No English.

AJ

Right. And my Spanish ain't exactly as good as it
should be for a resident of Florida. I just started talking
really loud, and putting an O at the end of every word.
Didn't seem to work as far as communication, but did
manage to be a little insulting. I guess that's
something.

CHRIS

Claim victory in the part of the field.
*(He takes off his jacket and feels a bulge in the inside
pocket. He pulls out a pack of Gummy Bears.)*
Hey, hey! My Gummy Bears from the movies last
week! Yes, Virginia, there is a Santa Clause.
(He opens the pack.)

AJ

What movie did we see? I forget.

CHRIS

No you didn't. I went by myself.

AJ

Very independent, my friend. Where was I?

CHRIS

*(He starts putting the Gummy Bears on the table. Some
around the coffee mug, some on top of the napkin
dispenser.)*
That was after the night we watched "The Good, The
Bad, and the Ugly" at like 4 in the morning, so you
slept until 6 the next day. I got up earlier than that, and
I had time to catch a movie. I bought the Gummy
Bears at a drug store by the theater so I wouldn't have
to pay eighty dollars inside, and as you can see, I just
forgot I had them.

AJ

And what are you doing with them now?

CHRIS

I'm having little Gummy West Side Story. I got the yellow and white ones over here, they're the Jets.
(Moving the Gummies around, singing.)
"When you're a Jet, you're a Jet all the way…"And over here I got the green and red ones as the PRs, with Maria and her sister up here.
(On top of the napkin dispenser. Singing, Spanish accent.)
"A boy like that, he kill your brother…"

AJ

(He picks up a Gummy Bear and eats it.)
You've got problems.

CHRIS

Hey, now I need a new lead, damn it. You just ate Tony.

AJ

You know he and Maria should be together.
(He reaches for the green Gummy Bear on top of the napkin dispenser.)

CHRIS

(Grabs one of the green ones)
Don't touch Maria.
(He holds the Gummy Bear close, singing to it.)
Maria, I just can't stop saying, Maria.
(AJ looks around his pockets.)

AJ

Hey, gimme a cigarette.

CHRIS

You had all those packs I was counting on you.

AJ

Well, they got 'em all.

CHRIS

Ah, Jesus, I'll run to the gas station.

AJ

Good, I gotta run to the bathroom.
(CHRIS leaves. AJ calls to AMY.)

Amy, can you watch my jacket a second.
(Close to her, standing by the counter.)
I don't exactly trust the Vienna Boys Choir over there.
AMY
No problem, A.

AJ
Thanks.
(AJ goes toward the back, off the stage, where the
bathroom would be.)
AMY
(To audience.)
These guys, they always focus on the negative. Lesley
Gore was an icon. Her songs will be remembered for
years. She's no Carole King, but along with her
repetitive lyrics in a story of high school sweethearts,
which everyone seems to throw in her face, she also
sang one of the first songs proclaiming women's
liberation. Her song "You Don't Own Me," was one of
the first feminist manifestos, I can't remember if that
came first or "I Am Woman." But the fact is, when
anyone talks about Lesley Gore, they only remember
the Judy/Johnny romance fiasco. I like that word,
"fiasco" I don't get to use it often. It sounds Italian.
Anyway, the song "You Don't Own Me" was a
breakthrough in a time when most songs were saluting
the inferiority of women. Like the song "Wishin' and
Hopin'" by Dusty Springfield, that song has a chorus
telling women to change themselves to get their man.
(Girly voice, singing.)
"Wear your hair, just for him, do the things he likes to
do." I thought we always taught our daughters that
they should always be themselves, but you got this
Springfield chick saying it's fine for them to be
themselves, but if they want a man, change everything.
Lesley's late work for the women's movement was an
in-your-face anthem that said, "Hey, you don't tell me
what to do, don't tell me what to say!" "I'll hang out

with who I want to, when I want to, and you can't do nothin' about it." Lesley was telling women that they run relationships, not men. While some women have difficulty grasping the concept, I think most have made good use of the information. Men get upset about this imbalance in relationships, but the only thing they can do about it is not get involved in the whole relationship process altogether. And though some hold out longer than others, they all fall eventually. Rest assured, there is no escaping…the puppet-masters.

(She motions her hands around like in a puppeteer motion.)
(AJ comes back from the bathroom.)

AJ
(To the cook, ARCHIE.)
Hey, Arch, where's the food, eh?

ARCHIE
You want to do this? Hey, was that a good game today or what?

AJ
FSU won by 30, Archie. That's not a good game. No, sports were meant to be exciting, nail-biting fights to the death, where the outcome of the game could be drastically changed at any minute, even at the last minute. That's why baseball's so great. It's a low scoring sport, so in any inning, any pitch could change the course of the game.

ARCHIE
Yeah, like hockey.

AJ
(He is sitting at his table now, rifling through CHRIS's little book as he talks.)
No, Arch, I said sports.

ARCHIE
You got a problem with hockey?

                    AJ
I got a problem with any athletic event dominated by
players from France and Canada.
                    AMY
Please, don't get him started on his hockey speech. I
heard him ramble about that for a good thirty minutes
one time. So, AJ, the people who picked FSU
today…Did you pay them off already?
                    AJ
You know, Amy, you'd know all about our operation if
you'd just place a bet every now and then.
                    AMY
                (Laughs.)
No thanks.
                    AJ
            (Darth Vader voice.)
It is your destiny. Come to the dark side.
                    AMY
I don't know anything about sports, AJ. Besides, what
money would I use? Food money? What am I gonna
tell my kid? "Sorry, Jaime, we can't eat this month.
The Packers couldn't cover the spread."
                    AJ
Gotta teach him disappointment somehow. But
anyway, today after the game we just collected. We
don't pay off till tomorrow. That way the money we
collect today can be used to pay off the winners and we
don't have to hit up Uncle Mike for cash. You've seen
us do this before.
    *(He pulls out a stack of empty envelopes from his
                    coat.)*
We take the cash we've collected, put it in the
envelopes, write the name of the payoff, and mark it all
down. Document everything.
        (He holds up CHRIS's little book.)
All that's left we hand over to Uncle Mike, at which
point he rewards us for our arduous work. And this is

                    141

what pays the bills and also provides for our lavish tastes.
(He motions around and points out his surroundings.)
(CHRIS walks back in and throws a carton of cigarettes to AJ.)
CHRIS
Cartons were discounted. We should be set for the week.
(He notices AJ is looking through his book.)
What are you looking for?
AJ
I was just explaining to Amy the intricacies of our operation.
CHRIS
It's really not that complicated. A monkey could do what we do.
AJ
But would they derive the same amount of pleasure from it? I think not.
CHRIS
Well, let me get that so I can start filling these things.
(He takes his envelopes out of his pocket.)
AJ
I'm gonna check on a mark. You know, that dentist guy...Phil Renkin. You remember I had to see him last month about that route canal. I'm hoping...
CHRIS
He lost $250 on the Gators.
AJ
Yes!
CHRIS
I had to meet him at his office to collect. He still doesn't tell his wife about his gambling.
(AJ hands him the book.)
AJ
Terrible thing to live in fear. Such is the life of the married man.

*(They are both seated now, filling their envelopes,
smoking.)*

Hey, I wanted to tell you, I test drove one of those new
VW bugs today.

CHRIS

What? Why? It's a clown car.

AJ

Hey, it's got personality. Besides, I wasn't gonna buy
it or anything. Harry Schiff, the car dealer, is one of
my guys. He dropped 300 on the game today and when
I went to see him, I test drove this new Beetle.

CHRIS

And...

AJ

It actually has a surprising amount of interior space.
And it had a little flower vase by the steering wheel,
which I think is pretty cool. Very 1960s, psychedelic
flower power kind of thing. Like I said, personality.
But get this: There is no lighter. No cigarette lighter!
They just got a port for plugging in a cell phone or
whatever, and there are no ashtrays. It's a non-smoking
car! I couldn't believe it. I must've ranted about that
for thirty minutes back at the dealership. They even
make a point of mentioning that in the owner's
manual. They're proud of it! Imagine a company so
politically motivated against smoking that they would
eliminate an entire market of people from buying their
car. But then what can you expect from the German's?
They wrote the book on political extremism.

CHRIS

So, just so I get this straight, because of the lack of an
ashtray or lighter in their new models, you're likening
the Volkswagen Company to the Nazi Party?

AJ

Hey, I looked it up my friend, the first Volkswagen
Bug rolled off the assembly line in Germany at the

behest of Hitler himself. The more things change, the more they stay the same.

(They each take out a large wad of money and place it next to their envelopes.)

CHRIS

I still think we shouldn't carry this kind of money around with us without some kind of protection. I think we should talk to Uncle Mike about that.

AJ

What? You want to start carrying a gun or something? You're not exactly Charles Bronson, Chris.

CHRIS

I know that, but maybe Uncle Mike can spare somebody on days like this, you know?

AJ

Relax, I have a full-proof plan for staying out of that kind of trouble. It's an exercise in psychology, really. I've actually gotten into the criminal mind. The typical mugger or stick-up artist, or whatever they call themselves, will not attack you if they think you're retarded.

CHRIS

What?

AJ

Think about it. The average criminal would be under the impression that a retarded person wouldn't have that much money on him in the first place. And second, they'd have to spend too much time explaining. A mugger doesn't want to have to spend twenty minutes clarifying the concept of robbery to a retard. So, whenever I feel like I'm in a threatening situation, I just drool on myself uncontrollably.

(He demonstrates, and drools on himself right there at the table.)

CHRIS

(Kind of disgusted, but also laughing, putting napkins underneath AJ's face.)

Ah, shit.

AJ

Then, I limp like my feet don't work, and walk down
the street trying to bite my face.
(He demonstrates this for a short while.)
All the while mumbling like Rain Man.

CHRIS

And that's your plan?

AJ

No muggings yet. Sometimes, while I'm doing this, if I
carry a cup, people put money in it.

CHRIS

You're unbelievable.

AJ

*(Stuffing envelopes with money, checking in his little
book.)*
Hey, where were you last night anyway? You didn't
answer your phone all night. There was a "Cheer's"
marathon on Nick at Nite.

CHRIS

Oh, shit, I missed it? Damn, did they have all the ones
with Harry Anderson?

AJ

Most of them. I settled in to watch the whole thing
during the course of the night, but it got old after a
while with no one there to watch it with me. I got so
restless during the fourth hour, I started shaving in
between the commercial breaks.

CHRIS

That's actually refreshing, though, isn't it? To have a
clean shave before you go to bed. I think it makes the
pillow feel softer.

AJ

I didn't shave my face, Chris.
(He scratches his crotch.)

CHRIS

Ahh, man, I can't leave you alone for five minutes, can I?

AJ

Well, because I only did it during commercial breaks, the whole operation took like forty minutes, and the shave won't be even since I did it in shifts.

CHRIS

I'll take your word for it. You know that's gonna grow out ten times more now, don't you? You're gonna have to either shave it consistently now, or buy pants a size larger to accommodate.

AJ

That's an old wives tale. Besides I'm not so worried about the growth back so much as the itching. I scratch more than a ball player now. I've tried various lotions, which is cool for a while, but doesn't much help in the long term.

CHRIS

I'm gonna have to lock up your shave kit now. You can't be trusted alone with it.

AJ

Well, why was I alone last night?

CHRIS

I was meeting with a client.

AJ

Client? I hate when you...What are we? Lawyers?

CHRIS

Fine. Okay, you want me to say it? I was meeting with a rube. Happy?

AJ

All night?

CHRIS

We had a lot in common. We talked for a while. Jesus, AJ, you sound as if you're jealous. I had a conversation with someone besides you. Call me crazy, I felt like broadening my horizons.

146

                          AJ
You're crazy.
            (AMY brings two plates of food for the guys.)
                         AMY
Well, I'm not really sure what to say here, fellas.
                          AJ
What do you mean?

                         AMY
Well, part of me wants to complain about your lack of
diversity, you know, always getting the same food all
the time. But the other part of me likes the fact that I
don't have to ask you all the time, "What'll it be
today?" And write some shit down. So, I'm not really
sure what to say. I feel like an actress who's forgotten
her lines.
                        CHRIS
You can't go wrong with "Enjoy."
                         AMY
I'll try.
        (She clears her throat as if about to deliver a big,
                        dramatic line.)
Enjoy.
                 (The guys applaud.)
                          AJ
Very nice.
         (She bows as she goes back to the counter.)
She's a natural. I actually believe she wants us to enjoy
our meal.
                        CHRIS
The great ones always make it seem so easy.
                     (As they eat.)
                          AJ
Oh, I almost forgot. How did the collection go with
that one girl?
                        CHRIS
    (He drops his fork as this last question is asked.)
What...what girl?

                          147

                        AJ
That dance team girl for the Magic. I bet she was mad,
eh? Was there swearing? Tell me there was swearing.
                      CHRIS
What are you talking about? I didn't have to collect
from her. She bet on the favorite.
                        AJ
                    (Thinking.)
No she didn't. She bet on the Gators. You said her ex-
boyfriend worked as a coach down at FSU, and that
was why she bet against them. Remember, we said we
were gonna drive down to the campus and take him out
to dinner.

                      CHRIS
No, she had 500 on FSU, that's why it wasn't such a
big deal. She bet on the favorite. And she's not a dance
team member anymore, she's in the marketing office.
                        AJ
I don't care...
          (He grabs CHRIS's little black book.)
                      CHRIS
What are you doing?
                        AJ
I'm checking on this mark. What was her last name?
De...something? Sounded Italian.
                (He rifles through the book.)
                      CHRIS
I don't even remember.
                        AJ
Here it is. Demarcos. I remember the first name.
                (He points it out to CHRIS.)
There it is, right there. Angela Demarcos. 500 on
Florida.

                      CHRIS
Maybe she called before the game and changed her
bet. You think of that before this inquisition?

AJ

What is this? What are you saying here? The story you
told was one of a woman scorned. She placed this bet
not because she knew anything about football, but
because she wanted to profit from something that was
painful to a guy that hurt her. People with those
motives don't change their bets at the last minute.
What are you telling me?

CHRIS

(After a pause.)

Don't be mad.

AJ

(Sputtering.)

Ahh, this...don't say that. I hate that. Just
say...Just...Tell me.

CHRIS

Last night, I was baking a cake. I knew about the
"Cheers" marathon, so I was gonna bring a cake over
to your place and we'd watch it. The marathon, not the
c...Well, during the baking process, I realize I have
nothing. I mean, I had the mix and the frosting...

AJ

What kind?

CHRIS

Betty Crocker. Yellow cake, milk chocolate icing. But,
I had no eggs, no flour for the pan...Not even any
milk. You can't have cake without milk. So, I ran to
the Food Way next to my place and while I was
picking up the various supplies...She was there.

AJ

Angela?

CHRIS

She was wearing a business suit, you know, very
professional. She had just gotten off of work and was
getting her groceries for the night. I don't understand
why people do that. Why get groceries for every night?
Normal people don't do that. You get a bunch of

groceries at the beginning of the month and there you go.

                    AJ
            (Visible grief.)
This was a conversation you had, wasn't it?
                  CHRIS
Yeah, that's how it all began.
        *(He gets up from the table and paces around,
            stuttering every other sentence.)*
I bumped into her in produce and we shopped together
and talked through all the aisles. We actually have a lot
in common. We talked about everything from current
events to our similar tastes in music, and when we got
to the checkout counter, we just decided to keep the
evening rolling. I told her I lived right next to the Food
Way, and I guess she felt comfortable enough with me
to...so we went...I poured some wine...and we made a
beef stir fry. The marinade was great, AJ, we started
with soy sauce for the base, then added...
    *(He notices the drastically uninterested look on AJ's
                    face.)*
Anyway the marinade was great. She added vegetables
which I personally felt was a mistake, mostly
because...

                    AJ
            (With grief.)
You hate vegetables.
                  CHRIS
Yeah. And so, when we finished with dinner and a few
more glasses of wine we baked the cake. When it was
in the oven, we sat on the couch and after a few more
drinks and random topics of conversation, we started
making ou...we started kissing. We did that for a
while, accompanied by various hand movements, then
the cake started burning. The smell is still lingering in
my apartment, AJ. We decided to call it a night, but...I
think there was something there, you know? As we

said our good-byes, I told her I'd really like to see her again…So, she's taking me to a Magic game on Monday. Courtside.

AJ
(Pointing at CHRIS's little book.)

And this?

CHRIS
(After a pause.)

Okay, don't get mad.

(AJ hits himself in the head with his hand in grief.)

I figured taking five hundred dollars away from someone was not the best way to begin a relationship. So I figured I'd tell her I put her money on FSU, pay her the winnings, which come out to a mere $250 dollars, and then all of a sudden I'm a romantic hero.

AJ

Chris, if you tell her you screwed up, you don't look like a hero, you look like an idiot, which is exactly what you are if you think Uncle Mike is just gonna forget about a five hundred dollar miss in your books with just a wink and a smile. The minute he thinks he can't trust you is the minute you lose this job…at the least. Remember two years ago, when Hank McCoy started feeding winnings to his aunt in Pensacola? Uncle Mike broke all the bones in his right hand and repossessed his aunt's car. Sure, we're not gangsters. You're not going to sleep with the fishes or wake up with a horse head in your bed, but with your personal life and methods of entertainment, I know you've become very fond of your hands.

CHRIS

Don't worry, alright. I'm not stupid enough to cheat Uncle Mike out of anything. And give me some credit, will you? I call him Uncle Mike for a reason. He trusts me with his business. He gave me a job right out of college working side by side with my best friend. We're a family, okay? I am familiar with the concept

151

of loyalty. I'm still gonna get him the money to cover this mark. It'll be just like she paid, and no one's the wiser.

CENTER>
                        AJ
This business was not meant to be a dating service, Chris. So, just to total it all up, you're going to cover her debt with us, and pay off her end out of your own pocket? That's $750 dollars.

                        CHRIS
I got stuff put away for a rainy day.
(The man at the counter, COUNTER MAN, leans back,
blatantly eavesdropping on their conversation.)

                        AJ
It ain't raining for this girl, Christopher. What are you gonna do if she keeps placing bets and keeps losing? You gonna be a hero to this girl right into the poorhouse? And Jesus, you spend a night doing the mattress mambo with a professional like Tina Koslowsky...

(He takes her card out of his wallet and throws it on
the table.)
...for three hundred dollars and she'll call you Spartacus if you ask her to. But you're willing to pay close to a grand for this girl over a few kisses and some strategically placed gropes. That's inflation.

                        CHRIS
Would you please stop trying to peddle your whores, AJ. You don't exactly have the wardrobe to be a pimp.

                        AJ
It just seems like a big risk for a product that you're not even sure is any good.
(COUNTER Man spins around in his chair and
interjects after this last comment.)
                   COUNTER MAN
That's actually a very good point. You wouldn't take out a loan to buy a car without test driving it first.

AJ

See? Listen to this guy. That's a pretty good analogy, pal.

COUNTER MAN

Well, not to brag, but I was an English major in college. You might say a metaphor comes as easy to me as a fine tune to a composer.

AJ

Now that's a simile, right?

COUNTER MAN

You're good.

CHRIS

(Sarcastic.)

That's great. Is this little meeting of the minds done here? Because at this particular moment, I don't really care about what your major was in college.

(COUNTER MAN is a little perturbed, but realizes his place and spins around away from the two.)

AJ

If this is about variety, we can ask Tina to suggest some new girls. Apparently she says the market is flooded. We'll have her rate the best ones for us, as far as looks, talent, flexibility...

CHRIS

Haven't you gotten it yet? This is not about sex. Sure, Ang has a great body, and I'd be lying if I told you getting naked with that body was not one of the things I want to do before I die, but this is more than that.

AJ

(Making a face.)

Ang?

CHRIS

I'm getting tired, A. I'm tired of going through the motions, pretending my life is perfect. I'm tired of just hearing about how adults live, or seeing it on television, all the while repeating to myself, "Don't need it. Not for me." You remember Leo Sullivan from

153

college? Got married right after graduation. He's got two kids in grade school and he called me the other night to tell me he's six months into having a third. That is real life, AJ. Backyard barbecues and playing catch in the front yard. Little league games and the PTA. That is how adults live. We've had our fun. We've lived our little independent lives. I think it's time to try a different road...and I'd like to try that road with Angela.

                              AJ
                      (After a pause.)
I don't believe this. I do not believe this. We had an agreement. We had an understanding.

                            CHRIS
I always find it amusing how you repeat yourself when you get flummoxed.

                              AJ
This is funny to you?

                            CHRIS
Actually, no. I gotta laugh to keep from crying. Most friends, especially best friends, would be happy that I met someone I consider special. Someone I like spending time with and enjoy the company of. When I tell you that I made out with an attractive woman back at my apartment, you're supposed to wink and nudge me with your elbow. We're supposed to exchange high fives and make a lot of stupid noises.
          (He imitates arrogant male noises.)
Ho ho ho. Heh heh heh.
  (The girls at the nearby table focus their attention on CHRIS and AJ's argument as their voices get louder and louder.)
                              AJ
In most cases, when this news comes, it doesn't come with the bonus report of how you're willing to risk your job and give up some major bank for this little make out session. Not to mention the fact that it throws

a monkey wrench into our whole philosophy of life.
But hey, if it'll make you feel better…
(He does some very exaggerated winking and nudging,
making noises sarcastically.)
Heh heh heh. High five.
(He puts his hand up as if to get a high five from
CHRIS.)
CHRIS
(Ignoring the high five.)
What is your problem with this? I've explained how
I'll handle the financial thing and Uncle Mike. I'm
very comfortable in the financial arena. Unlike some
people, not all my money goes towards the country's
largest collection of pornography. If this is genuine
concern, I appreciate it, but this sounds like there's
more involved here.

AJ
It's not…It's just…I don't want to see you get hurt. I
know I'm not your mother, but I remember how you
were all those nights after college, you coming to me,
whining about some girl you went out with who didn't
want another date. Or coming back from those God
awful dance clubs, wreaking of cheap perfume,
embarrassed that you just took part in that whole
scene. You have a tendency to get a very high-pitched
voice when you whine, you know that? This is just an
attempt to prevent you from inflicting that pain on me
again. And as for this girl, what do you even really
know about her? You're talking about a woman you've
known for about a week, have gone out with once, and
already you're spending close to a thousand dollars
trying to go down some metaphorical road with her. If
I wasn't here to try and protect you from yourself who
knows how many other women you'd just hand money
to.

CHRIS

Would you get off the money thing, please! We've already established that that is not the issue.
(One of the girls from the table, TESS, comes over to the guys at this point. The other girl, HOLLY, comes close, but does not approach the table. She just sits at a counter seat close to the action.)

TESS

If you guys are arguing over a woman, you really shouldn't. Friendships are too important to be torn apart over such things. We're a dime a dozen, really.
(She chuckles.)
For the good ones...four for a quarter.

COUNTER MAN
(Spinning around and butting in.)
It's not like that, exactly. You see, it is over a woman, but not in the sense of what you're thinking. This guy here...
(Pointing at CHRIS.)
...is involved with a woman, apparently a high-priced lady, and this guy here...
(Pointing at AJ.)
...doesn't think she's worth it.

AJ

Doesn't anybody mind their own business anymore?

CHRIS

Listen. Mole people. We appreciate your concern, but my woman problems are my busi...are our business. So, if you don't mind...
(He motions for them to leave.)

TESS

Alright, I got what I needed.
(She puts out here hand to HOLLY. HOLLY hands her a twenty dollar bill.)
Men arguing over women. A sure bet.
(TESS walks back to her table. As HOLLY is about to do the same, AJ stops her.)

AJ

What did you think we were arguing about?

HOLLY

A man.

(She then walks back to her table.)

AJ

You see? It's your high-pitched voice that leads to misconceptions like that.

CHRIS

Would you please just tell me what this is all about? You don't know anything about this girl and already you've got her developing some elaborate plan to bankrupt me.

AJ

Where do you go from here? You've had one dinner and one "great" conversation, which, by the way, was facilitated by alcohol. So sober, this girl might be as interesting as a documentary on Wisconsin.

COUNTER MAN

(Spinning around again.)

Another simile. But hey, man, I'm from Wisconsin and I don't appreciate...

CHRIS

(Ignoring him.)

AJ, what are you afraid of? And don't say you don't want me to get hurt, because you relish every chance you get to say, "I told you so."

AJ

I very rarely relish things.

CHRIS

Now you're just avoiding the subject.

AJ

Alright, fine. You want to know why I hate this situation? You want the truth? Okay, you're right. I don't care if you get hurt. You're a big boy, I'm not going to hold your hand while you make the mistakes that affect your life. And you're right, I do like saying,

157

"I told you so." This is not about you trying this relationship with this girl and failing. That I can live with. I've got a problem with what happens if this relationship goes as far as you currently hope it will.

CHRIS

Like you know.

AJ

Contrary to what you might believe, I do listen to you from time to time. Your little schpiel about how adults live…having kids and Little League and what not…it's not coincidental that you have this great night with this one chick and the next day you're talking about the PTA. I'm not afraid of you shooting the moon and coming up short…I'm afraid…one day…you're gonna make it.

CHRIS

Why…

AJ

What's wrong with what we got here, eh? This is great. You're right, this is not how adults live. But that's what's so great about it! This…

(He points out the surroundings.)

…is fun. You talk about your backyard barbecues with suburban neighbors, your kids and your wife, but nobody has fun with those things. If you're lucky, your kids will only disrespect you. Some parents have to worry about kids who become pyromaniacs, kleptomaniacs, drug users or drug pushers and even some children who get their kicks shooting up a school. With wives, at best she'll only shop you into the poorhouse. Of course, she could always cheat on you, destroying your already fragile self-confidence. Or, for laughs, she'll just cut off your penis while you're sleeping.

CHRIS

Now that's not fair. The Bobbitt thing is off limits! You are not allowed to bring that up with another guy!

158

That's the ultimate trump card. We've got no response for that.

CENTER: AJ

And as for suburbia on the whole…Neighborhood politics are the worst. Pot luck picnics and block parties and bridge clubs. All that phony greeting bullshit in the mornings or afternoons. "Hey, Bill, you working hard or hardly working?" Everybody sticking their noses in everybody else's business, without paying enough attention to their own. You'll get people telling you to clean up your yard, trim your hedges, or mow your lawn…all for the sake of the community. Total strangers will tell you how to take care of your property, and they'll do it in the most contemptible ways. "Whoa, Chris, grass getting a little high there, isn't it?" And all the while, the wife harping at you to do what they say, because she doesn't want to be embarrassed when they bring up the "Malone Savanna" at the next block party. It's all phony, Chris. When people get married, they forget how to have fun, so they pretend that everything is fun, while complaining about it at the same time. And despite this hellish existence, you'll go to bed each night with a giant, shit-eating grin, and thank the Lord you got married and had kids, because now you're complete. That's what success leads to in these romantic endeavors of which you speak.

CENTER: CHRIS
(After a pause.)

It's sad that this is a speech that we have made before. Hearing it now, it is pretty damn sad that we have inflicted this on other people.

CENTER: AJ

It's fucking heartbreaking that I have to give it to you now, after having to beat it into your head oh so many years ago! This is a hurdle we overcame, Malone! We are happy…genuinely happy…with our current

lifestyle. You and me. No need for anyone else. And
yet even after only one dinner in two meetings with
this Angela person, you'll say, "It'll be different for us.
We won't act like that." The anthem of all people on
the cusp of a relationship. Well, you're already in a
relationship, Chris. And it is different for us, and we
don't act like that. You're so wrapped up in trying to
get involved in something with this girl, you disregard
the time we've spent trying to build this relationship.
Well you've got all the answers, Answer Man, what
happens to me when you embark on this little road-trip
with Ms. Demarcos? What happens to me when you're
at your block parties and PTA meetings?

CHRIS

This is not about you!

AJ

Oh, you've gotta learn the rules of a relationship if you
want to get involved with a woman, my friend.
Because they know all of them and there are daily
quizzes. Rule number one is that when something
affects one member of the relationship, it also affects
the other. So you've explained to me what you plan to
get out of your new life with this new person: Little
League and mini van and so on…So, how will it affect
me?

CHRIS

I still don't understand the question. I'm not asking
you to change at all. You can go right on being the
stubborn, unwavering son of a bitch that you've always
been. We'll still hang out. I'm getting involved with a
woman, AJ. I'm not dying.

AJ

Dying I could accept. You wouldn't make a conscious
decision to die. And don't say "We'll hang out,"
because that's bullshit. At this point in our friendship
we are not merely two people who "hang out."

Besides, in the one night you went out with this girl,
we've already missed out on a major event.
                    CHRIS
              (Interrupting. Flabbergasted.)
It was a "Cheer's" marathon, for Christ's sake!
                      AJ
                (Still rolling.)
And stuff like that is just the beginning. What's going
to happen if she doesn't like me? She is going to try to
discourage you from spending time with me. Then
you'll have to sneak away to come "hang out" with
me. And shit like this…
         (He motions again to his surroundings.)
…mindless chatter in the middle of the night with Amy
and Archie, you can kiss that good-bye. She's gonna
want you to be with her all night, talking about life or
whatever.
   *(He then acts as if something extraordinary has just
                  donned on him.)*
And I bet she doesn't smoke either, does she?
                    CHRIS
Actually…no.

                      AJ
I knew it! I knew it! She is going to make you quit! I
swear to God! She is going to make you quit, that
manipulative bitch! Watch. It'll start out with
something small. She'll tactfully cover her face with a
scarf or handkerchief when you smoke around her,
because she doesn't like the smell. Then, out of
respect, you'll stop smoking around her. Then, she
won't want you to smoke where you live, because the
smell lingers in the house. Then, she won't let you be
around people who smoke, because the smoke stays in
your clothes. So right there I'm out of the picture. And
finally, she won't want you to smoke at all because she
hates the way the smoke tastes when she kisses you.
Before you know it, I'm gonna need a picture of you in

my wallet to remember what you look like, and you'll be one of those bastards in the non-smoking section complaining about secondhand smoke.

CHRIS

You already have a picture of me in your wallet, remember? That one we took at Coney Island when…

AJ

This is not the point. The point is we are already in a relationship. A damn good one. One built on mutual tastes and personalities…and smoking. You can tell me anything, and I can tell you anything. There isn't one problem we've ever had in our lives that we couldn't smoke our way out of. You say you and Angela have a lot in common, well what the hell am I? We're practically the same person, you and I, and yet you're bending over backwards for a girl who you think has a few things in common with you.

CHRIS

You're telling me you've never wanted to see what the whole family situation was like for yourself? You've never wanted to see what's on the other side of the fence?

AJ

I don't have to, Chris. And neither do you. People look for things on the other side because they are unhappy with their current situations. We're doing great. The only reason you're contemplating it now is because you felt the good part of it for a few brief moments. I love spending all my time in the smoking sections of all these places we've come to enjoy. And I love spending that time with my best friend. I love staying up to all hours in the night talking about meaningless shit. That's what our lives consist of…meaningless shit. No crises, no catastrophes. We're just two regular guys, Chris, and because we realize that and accept our place in the universe, we have the ability to just be. We're not concerned with global warming or political unrest in Haiti, but we cry like babies if we miss a rerun of "Law & Order." And you want to go from that to raising a family? In an average family, everything is a crisis. "I didn't get that promotion at work." "The Smith's down the street said our dog bit their son." "Little Johnny won't get the toy he wants for Christmas this year." All that drama. All that shit. You can't leave me for that, Chris. Please don't leave me for that. Without this, what do I have?

CHRIS
(Timid.)

You...You could try it too, you know? It might not be so bad. We could double date and go places together. If we had kids they could grow up together...be best friends all their lives. You could be Uncle AJ and I would be Uncle Chris...We'd do that thing where we pull quarters out of their ears.

AJ

The only thing that would pull us apart more than one of us with a woman would be both of us with a woman. Your family pulls you one way, my family pulls me another. That fantasy never comes true. We live our fantasy now. We are best friends who spend every free moment together, hindered by nothing. We have more fun than anyone over the age of 12. This is really the first serious conversation we've ever had. The runner up would have to be that religious discussion we had a week ago.

CHRIS
(He is puzzled at first, then he remembers.)

Oh, you mean when you thought that Jesus would be better in bed than the devil?

AJ

Yeah. And you were convinced that Satan was a better lay because he was more violent, and he'd do more kinky stuff. I still stand behind Jesus, though. After all,

163

it's his name that most people call out in times of
passion.
>   *(He then imitates an orgasm.)*
"Oh, Jesus! Oh, Christ!"
>   *(He laughs.)*
There was a priest sitting next to us when we had that
discussion, remember?
>   CHRIS
You asked him if he could settle the argument.
>   AJ
And, boy, the things he said to me. Whew…I can't
believe what God lets his employees get away with
nowadays.
>   CHRIS
My favorite conversation was at that steakhouse when
you asked if it would be less of a social taboo to have
sex with a 13-year old or an 84-year old.
>   AJ
The mother at the table beside us hit me with her
purse. Twice.
>   CHRIS
They had to move her and her kids to another part of
the restaurant.
>   AJ
That hurt like a bitch, man, she must've had like a
brick in her purse or something.
>   *(He rubs his head in nostalgic pain.)*
But those are the things we do. Those are the times we
have. Don't trade those in for a chick, man. Don't trade
me in for some chick and the PTA.
>   CHRIS
>   *(After a long pause.)*
Well, I would save close to eight hundred dollars…
>   AJ
>   *(Lifts up Tina Koslowski's card from the table.)*
That's like three full nights with Tina.

CHRIS
(Slowly.)
You sure you can't get me an AJ discounted price?
(He takes the card.)
AJ
For you, bud, anything.
*(Looks down to the black book, which is still opened to
Angela's page.)*
This was a scary conversation, my friend. I don't mind
telling you...
(Pause.)
I gotta splash some water on my face here, get back to
reality.
(He gets up from the table.)
Of course, you realize this means you're stuck with
me. Just little ol' me.
CHRIS
I wouldn't have it any other way. And hey, we can
always crash the occasional PTA meeting if we want.
We can pretend to be some kids parents...a kind of
"My Two Dads" sort of thing.
AJ
Sounds fun. But you have to be the uptight, Paul
Reiser-dad, and I get to be the other guy...The cool
dad. Who played him?
CHRIS
Greg Evigan. I wonder what ever happened to him.
AJ
I think he replaces Archie behind the grill on the day
shift.
*(They both laugh at the perceived misfortune of the
great actor, Greg Evigan.)*
CHRIS
(After a pause.)
This was...It was just a temporary lapse, AJ. Just a
momentary phase.

AJ

*(Still standing, he holds the black book in his hand still
on Angela's page. He looks down at it.)*
This phase scared the hell out of me, Chris. This
girl...she almost did it. She almost took my best friend
away from me.
(He hands him the book still open.)
Now, I can trust you with this, right? I won't have to
burn this entry or anything, will I?

CHRIS

You can leave the entry. Don't worry, I'm not
that...Well, you can leave the number but I think
you'd better collect the debt. Just promise you'll
behave.

AJ

I'll try. No promises, though.
*(He pulls a pack of cigarettes out of his pocket, hands
CHRIS a cigarette, then lights it.)*
I'm glad you're still with us.

CHRIS

Just a phase, man. Just a phase.
*(AJ walks back to the bathroom. CHRIS is left sitting
there with the black book open to Angela's number in
one hand and Tina Koslowsky, the prostitute's number
in the other. He looks back and forth between the two,
still smoking. He then takes out his cell phone and
looks back to where AJ walked to, checking to make
sure he wasn't coming, then he dials.)*

CHRIS

(On the phone.)
Yes, hello? Hi, this is Chris...Chris Malone. Yeah. I'm
sorry to call so late, but...Oh, you were? Good...I was
hoping...Anyway, I was wondering if it would be
possible...if you weren't busy...if you could meet me
tonight. It's been a long day and...Great. Do you
remember how to get to my place? Yeah, that's right.

Right next to the Food Way. Okay, great. I'll see you then.
(Pause, still on the phone. He is about to hang up but just then thinks of something else.)
Oh…and Tina…Just for tonight, for no particular reason…Could you call me Spartacus? Thanks.
(He hangs up, and continues smoking, but after a brief pause he confronts the audience.)
What? Who did you think it was?
(The scene closes to Leslie Gore's "You Don't Own Me.")

END SCENE 1

SCENE 2—*The Alamo. This is a Texas Steakhouse. It has picnic tables and wooden booths as its décor, with a lot of neon signs hanging on the walls. Beer signs mostly. There are a mess of peanut shells on the ground, with faint sounds of pleasant country music. The entrance is on one side of the stage, with a cardboard cow holding a sign that says, "Ya'll wait to be seated, now." There are three booths lined up along the main stage. There is a family of four, two parents and two young girls, JOSIE and GRACIE, sitting at the table on the far right, and JAMES from SCENE 2, and a new girl STEPH, are sitting in the booth on the far left. STEPH is a gorgeous young girl to rival SCENE 2's TIFFANY. JAMES is wearing the same outfit from SCENE 2. There are buckets of peanuts on each table. A young hostess, CINDY LOU, in country clothes, is writing in a book at the front by the cow sign. CHRIS is also at the front by the cow, wearing the same football jersey and running pants he wore in SCENE 3, carrying his jacket in his hand, pacing back and forth.*
CHRIS
(To the audience, very jittery, still pacing.)
I'm…I'm calm. I'm keeping my head. I am cool. I am a rock. Steady, cool, composed.
(He puts his hand out in front of him to make sure it is steady, just like an old gunfighter. It is indeed steady.)

Alright, alright. Now, this is weird. I'm not really sure
how I'm supposed to handle this. Don't get me wrong,
I know how to handle confrontation. I've done it
before, and pretty damn well, I gotta tell ya. One time
at McDonald's, I asked for no pickle on my burgers,
and I got a pickle…Whooo…That kid behind the
counter had no idea what hit him. I actually made him
cry, 15-year-old punk. And when I ask for a Coke with
no ice…There ain't one cube, not one cube, if the staff
knows what's good for it. But this is AJ. This is the
King of Confrontation. He knows all my buttons, and
exactly when to press them…and I always back off.
But this is something I feel strongly about, damn it. I
just have to stick with it, and remember not to let my
emotions get the best of me.

(He thinks for a minute.)

Or…am I supposed to use my emotions to amplify my
point…I've heard it both ways. It's like that good
cop/bad cop routine cops do in interrogation scenes.
One cop is given cart blanche and can act with open
animosity towards the suspect, while the other is
supposed to remain calm, like he's the guy's friend and
all. Well, I'm not really sure if I can do that whole
routine, but I can imitate one portion of the
interrogation process. See, the main ingredient in all
the tough cop shows, like "NYPD Blue," "Homicide:
Life on the Street," or "Starsky and Hutch," was an
uncomfortable setting for the questioning. They never
questioned the suspect in comfortable environs. They'd
always put them under the hot lights, or put them in the
box…put them in an atmosphere that they found
totally unbearable.

(He gestures to his surroundings, smiling big.)

Enter the Alamo. Genuine Texas cuisine for the best in
family dining.

*(AJ then walks in the door and sees CHRIS waiting for
him.)*

168

                        AJ
Alright, alright. I'm here. Why are we trying this new
place anyway? Do we know anybody here? Who's the
manager? Who's the host?
            (He looks around the place.)
Why is there a cow at the entrance?
                      CHRIS
Relax, AJ. Now, I know you like routine. I know new
things aren't really your...thing. But I heard good
things about this place and I realize that there are few
places we go to that offer genuinely good barbecue.
And we love barbecue. Pulled pork, sirloin tips, baked
beans and a loaded baked potato...Hey, from what I
hear, my man, this place has a baked potato like you
wouldn't believe.

                        AJ
Chris, it's a potato. Not a lot of thought goes into its
preparation. And what is this you're wearing? Is
that...Are those the same clothes you were wearing the
other night? Is this the new look for you? Same clothes
over and over?

                      CHRIS
            (Eager to change the subject.)
Listen, I got a $30 dollar gift certificate to this place,
so everything's on me. You can't beat the price. Just
promise you'll give it a shot, okay? I told your mother
I'd make you try new things.

                        AJ
Alright, I'll give it a shot. How is my mother anyway?
                      CHRIS
Doing fine. She sends her love. Now, promise me
you'll give this place a legitimate chance. No faces, no
attitude.

                        AJ
Jesus, I promise, alright? Stop babying me and let's
just eat.
            (Now to the hostess.)

Excuse me.

CINDY LOU

(She has a heavy Texas Southern accent.)

Well, howdy, darlin's. Welcome to the Alamo. Family dinin' and Southern hospitality served from 10 to 10 every day. How can I help you?

AJ

(Visibly annoyed by her Texas ways, and mocking her with a bad, phony drawl.)

Yeah, darlin'. Could we just get a table for two in smoking, please?

CINDY LOU

(Waving a finger at him.)

Now, now. Remember the Alamo's slogan. Family dining in a family atmosphere. We like for the young ones to be able to eat here and not have to worry about that harmful secondhand smoke. We ain't got a smoking section, sugar.

AJ

Okay, thank you. Sorry we wasted your time. Ready, C-Man?

(He heads for the exit, but CHRIS grabs his arm.)

CHRIS

Now, wait a minute. You said you'd give this place a chance. I want pulled pig, I've been hungry for it all day. We're here...Let's just forgo the cancer sticks for one night, eh? We'll smoke a couple afterwards on the way to the car.

AJ

Chris, you know how I feel about these places...

CHRIS

Well, I didn't know it was that kind of place.

(He smiles to the audience.)

But we're here and maybe we can get an inside track as to what these non-smoking people are all about. It'll give us a little insight as to what these people are made of.

AJ

It's not like there's a big secret, buddy. They don't like smoke. End of story. Now, let's get out of here. I haven't had a cigarette since I was out in the car.

CHRIS

Look, I've got the certificate, we're here, we're hungry, they have food. Let's just spend an hour in each other's company, share a meal, have a good conversation, focusing on nothing in particular, and try not to miss the smoke. Let's live for a brief moment in the world of the people we loathe. It'll be a whole new perspective.

AJ

(Fed up.)

Alright, alright. Fine let's do it. Let's just do it. Let's sit down and get it over with. I'm tired of this whole conversation. You're hell-bent on eating here, we'll stay. But I want you to know I object to this whole meal with every fiber of my being. I may eat, but I won't enjoy.

CHRIS

So much for promises. Alright, let's eat.

AJ

(To CINDY LOU.)

We'll have a table for two in your section-less eatery, please.

CINDY LOU

Right this way, please.

(She leads them to the middle booth. AJ walks to his seat but notices the neon beer signs hanging around.)

AJ

Family restaurant, eh?

(He points to one of the signs.)

But you sell liquor though, right?

CINDY LOU

Yes, sir. Full bar.

AJ

Oh, so any alcoholic father can come in here and get blatto drunk, vomit all over the place, take his kids home, beat the hell out of them and pass out naked in his driveway, but…

(He puts back on his country accent.)

…Hell's Bells, God forbid he light a cigarette, which to my knowledge, has never caused anyone to beat the hell out of anyone. Now that must be Texas logic.

(JAMES finally sees the two as AJ makes this statement.)

JAMES

(To STEPH, very panicked.)

Get your coat.

STEPH

But…

JAMES

No time. Get your coat.

(He gets up fast and grabs some money out of his wallet, throwing it on the table. AJ, now seated, sees him.)

AJ

Hey, look. It's that kid.

CHRIS

(Pivoting himself to see JAMES.)

James! Hey, James!

JAMES

(To himself more than to STEPH.)

Must hurry. No time.

(Now to STEPH.)

Ready? Good.

(He takes her hand and pulls her out of the restaurant while she only has her jacket half on.)

CHRIS

Must have had to be somewhere.

(To the hostess.)

Any specials?

AJ

Yeah, like is Monday like special smoking day?

CHRIS

Shut up. Behave. You promised.

CINDY LOU

Your waitress should be here shortly with all that
information. In the meantime, ya'll enjoy our
complementary peanuts, and when your friends ask
you about a good place to eat…Remember the Alamo.
(She goes back to her hostess counter by the big cow.)

AJ

She doesn't even know the specials?
(He shakes his head.)
Lack of professionalism.
*(He then gets very uncomfortable, and begins fidgeting
in his chair.)*

CHRIS

So, how did the payouts go yesterday? I'm still a good
deal ahead.
(He begins admiring his Rolex watch.)
Uncle Mike could've gotten us two Rolex's.

AJ

What is it with these booths? Are you uncomfortable? I
feel like I'm on a slab at the morgue.

CHRIS

Did you take care of all your payoffs yet?

AJ

Not all of them. Not yet.
*(He sees the family at the booth next to them, and he
sees one of them throw their peanut shells on the floor.
He then pays closer attention to the floor, noticing that
everyone throws their peanut shells down there.)*
Can you believe this? They won't let us smoke, but
they'll let you throw peanut shells on the floor? What
kind of message are they sending to the kids? This is
supposed to be a family restaurant. Sure, maybe the
kids that come here won't smoke when they get older,

173

but in the meantime, when they get home, they're
gonna throw all their garbage on the floor. I'd rather
have a kid smoking in the boy's room than trashing up
my living room.

CHRIS

(Getting angry, feeling ignored.)

Hey, focus! I'm asking you a question. This is
business! Now, why didn't you get the books taken
care of? Problems finding people?

AJ

Chris, I don't go looking for people. We set up
meetings in designated places, you know that. I'm not
gonna run around the city, seeking people out, that's a
waste of my time.

CHRIS

So why didn't you take care of your people? What
caused the delay?

AJ

(Still fidgeting in his chair.)

Do they even have a wait staff here? Or does
everybody just belly up to troth, Texas style?

CHRIS

Who did you take care of?

AJ

I got most everybody in the books, I just had a delay
with one person. Took a little longer than I expected.

CHRIS

Really? Who?

AJ

You have something you'd like to ask me, Chris? You
seem like you're taking the long way to get to a point
here, and I think I know what it is. So just trust me
when I say, you don't want to go there.

*(He takes out a pack of cigarettes, takes out a
cigarette, and puts it in his mouth.)*

I mean it. Drop it.

174

CHRIS

Hey, don't do me any favors, pal. Just tell me what happened with…

(The waitress, an older woman named LESLIE, comes up just then, interrupting the exchange. She is singing legend Leslie Gore.)

LESLIE

Howdy, fellas. Welcome to the Alamo. My name's Leslie and I'll be…

(She notices the cigarette in AJ's mouth.)

Whoa, buckaroo, remember the Alamo's policy on smoking?

AJ

Listen, Leslie, I'm not going to light it, alright? Just relax.

(He looks up into her face, and studies it. He then recognizes her.)

Wait a minute. Are you…You're Leslie Gore, aren't you?

LESLIE

(Blushing at the recognition.)

Yes, sir. I most assuredly am.

CHRIS

Wow, really? Leslie Gore? Holy shit.

LESLIE

You know you're a tragic story when people see you in a job like this and are automatically inspired to swear.

CHRIS

No, it's not that…Well, as long as we're on the subject…What the hell are you doing as a waitress here at the Alamo?

LESLIE

Thank you for putting it so delicately.

AJ

Well, you gotta admit…

LESLIE

No offense, no offense. Like many mega superstars of
my generation, I made the mistake of trusting all of my
money with people I shouldn't have trusted with even
a bus pass. It sort of all frittered away…as did many of
my talents. But hey, I had a few good years, didn't I?
And I can still sling hash with the best of them.

AJ

Well…

LESLIE

What?

AJ

I don't know about mega superstar. That's a bit
much…

LESLIE
(Interrupting.)
So what is it you fellas want to drink?

CHRIS

Jeez, Leslie Gore right here as our waitress. Hey, can
you do us a favor? I know you probably get this a lot…

LESLIE

You want like an autographed picture or something?

CHRIS

No, nothing like that. No, I was wondering, can you
repeat your waitress lines here three times like you did
with the lyrics in your songs? Like…
*(He begins singing these next lines just like the song
"Judy' Turn to Cry.")*
"What'll you have to drink? What'll you have to
drink? What'll you have to drink?"

LESLIE
(She is offended.)
Now wait just a minute…

AJ
(Calming her down.)
I'm sorry, ma'am. He's just teasing, that's all. You
can't blame him for trying.

LESLIE

Well, alright then…

AJ

After all, it's our table…
*(He now sings these next lines like "It's My Party and
I'll Cry If I Want To.")*
…we can try what we want to, try what we want to, try
what we want to…

LESLIE

(Very upset, yelling to the back of the restaurant.)
We need a different waitress for Table 5!
(She then storms away.)

CHRIS and AJ

(Singing after her.)
You would try to if it happened to you.

AJ

Oh, how the somewhat mighty have fallen.

CHRIS

Yeah, it's hard to belie…
*(He catches himself feeling too good, interrupts
himself and slaps AJ on the arm.)*
You bastard…You don't get to change the subject
here.

AJ

Not even for Leslie Gore?

CHRIS

We were discussing something very serious here, and I
think you have something to say to me.

AJ

Look Chris, the only reason you'd be pressing this
issue about the paybacks is because you think you
know something about the whole Demarcos thing. But
let me assure you, no matter what you think you know,
you don't know the truth, and it would be best if you
didn't.

CHRIS

Why don't you let me be the judge of what's best for me. Just tell me what I want to hear. Tell me what happened.

AJ

Alright…fine…
(He looks around, then lights the cigarette that was in his mouth. One of the little girls at the next table, GRACIE, sees this.)
What happened was…

GRACIE
(She is pointing and yelling at AJ.)
Mommy! Daddy! Smoker! Smoker!
(The other little girl chimes in.)
JOSIE and GRACIE
Smoker! Smoker!

AJ

Jesus, they've got spies everywhere!
(To the girls.)
No, shhh, no listen…
(CINDY LOU, LESLIE, and two other members of The Alamo staff surround their table. LESLIE is still really pissed.)
ALAMO STAFF
Now, partner, Remember the…
AJ
Alright, fine!
(He puts out the cigarette and throws it on the floor.)
There! Happy? Just enough of that "Remember the Alamo" crap! You know what the Alamo was all about? The Texans wanted to be independent of Mexico so they could add another slave state to the South, which the Mexicans didn't agree with. It wasn't a daring display of heroism and bravery. Davy Crockett was fighting to turn Kunta Kinte into Chicken George. That's your precious Alamo!

(The ALAMO STAFF leaves, a little frightened. But LESLIE stays behind, and she picks up AJ's pack of cigarettes and crushes them right in front of him and throws them on the ground and steps on them. She then leaves.)

AJ

(After a pause, looking down at his crumpled pack.)
I think we pissed her off.

CHRIS

Well, on the bright side…
(He leans down and picks up the crumpled pack.)
…you might be able to sell this as Rock and Roll memorabilia on EBay. "Authentic pack of cigarettes stepped on by Leslie Gore." Some of this shit goes up to a high price. I once saw…
(He notices he's gone off track again, and slaps AJ on the arm again.)
Stop trying to avoid the subject.

AJ

Listen, I didn't mean for it to happen, I swear. I just went to collect the debt.

CHRIS

I knew it! You couldn't resist, could you? You had to do it! But you know what? I knew you would. I expected as much. That's why I followed you. I saw the whole thing!

AJ

You saw…

CHRIS

Well, I didn't see the actual act. I didn't need to take pictures. I followed you to Angela's house, and then I spent the night in my car waiting for you to leave…Which you didn't do until eight this morning! That's why I'm wearing these funky clothes still. So, how was she? Better than a pro? Has she got a nighttime career ahead of her or what? Did you fulfill all your dance team fantasies? I bet you even made her

put on her old dance outfit, didn't you? You fucking
bastard!
*(He notices he cursed pretty loud, so he apologizes to
the family next to them.)*
Sorry.
                              AJ
                 (Leaning in, speaking low.)
You think... You think I slept with her?
                            CHRIS
Don't try to play this off, AJ! I was outside her place
all night! You guys weren't playing Scrabble! Did you
make her call you "Daddy"? Was she sore in the
morning?
                              AJ
                (Very remorseful. Very quiet.)
Ang... Angela is dead.
                            CHRIS
Yeah, right! Like you're that good...
                              AJ
                   (Still gravely serious.)
No, Chris... We didn't... There was no sex... She's just
dead. But I swear it was an accident.
                            CHRIS
*(Calming down, but still a little skeptical. He's getting
                       scared, though.)*
Are you serious? Don't joke about this, damn it! Are
you serious? What happened?
                              AJ
I called her from a pay phone outside of Leo's... I had
finished most of my payoffs for the day, so I thought
I'd take care of that one collection before I called it a
night. When I called, she thought I was you on the
phone, so I pretended to be you, so I could surprise her
in person and bitch her out for trying to seduce
you... for trying to tear us apart...
                            CHRIS
It wasn't a matter of seduction... What happened?

                             180

                    AJ

So, when I got there, I told her I was there to collect,
and she asked where you were and how come you
weren't collecting. So I said, "You'd like to know that
wouldn't you, bitch?" And she got this big attitude
problem. I told her to keep her hooves to herself, that
she wasn't welcome in our lives, and she got in my
face, pointing her finger at me, calling me all kinds of
names…and blah blah blah. And then she pushed me,
and kept shoving me backwards, trying to push me out
of the house. Well, you know I don't like to be
pushed…So I pushed her back…I pushed her
hard…and she's…she was just so little…she flew
backwards, lost her footing and cracked her head on
the coffee table. Her eyes were still open, and blood
was just pouring out of a big gash in her forehead.
There was no pulse.

                  CHRIS
                  (Slow.)

Oh, Jesus. Oh, Jesus.

                    AJ

I freaked out. I'd never been around a death before, let
alone the cause of one. I was so scared, Chris. People
get convicted of accidental deaths all the time, I didn't
know what to do. So…I called Uncle Mike.

                  CHRIS

You didn't call an ambulance? The police? 911?

                    AJ

She was dead, Christopher. There was nothing those
people could do. All that would have done was invite
them to come and arrest me. Uncle Mike told me to
clean the whole place, everything I might've touched.
He had me wipe up my footprints off of the hardwood
floors and make sure there were no traces of any part
of me on her body, so I had to clean off the spot on her
wrist where I checked her pulse. Everything was
dusted off. Then he told me to go to the cupboard and

                    181

get a bottle of vegetable oil, open it, and drop the bottle
on the floor, make it look like she'd slipped. Then, he
said to wait till early the next morning and walk out
like nothing had happened.

CHRIS
(His head is in his hands.)
Now…Now what?

AJ
Well, the original plan was not to tell you. Uncle Mike
was just gonna send us up to New York to work for a
guy he knows up there. I know you love New York, so
I knew you'd be good to go, no questions. Uncle Mike
said we'd only have to stay up there for like four
months, then by the time we came back, everything
would be fine.

CHRIS
Wait a minute. You weren't even going to tell me?
Jesus, AJ, I could be a suspect. I was the one who she
called to place the bet. She winds up dead after placing
a losing bet with me, that makes me a pretty good
suspect, don't you think?

AJ
Uncle Mike was going to say he sent us up to New
York right after the game, early in the day. We both
would've been cleared. I wouldn't hang you out to dry.
We were gonna go through it together.

CHRIS
What are we gonna do in New York?

AJ
Same thing we do here. Uncle Mike's friend works out
of the Aqueduct. We could watch the races all day,
work all night, do up the city every chance we get.
Think about it. Knick's games in the Garden. Big East
College Basketball. Baseball in Yankee Stadium. We'd
take in the same amount of money, and Uncle Mike
would bankroll us to start.

CHRIS

And you're sure you dusted off everything, right?
There's nothing that leads them to you?

AJ

Nothing. Uncle Mike talked me through the whole
thing. He seemed familiar with the process.

CHRIS

Alright, we catch the train for New York tomorrow.
We pack light, a few suits, some shorts, various
intangibles...We'll buy all the rest when we get up
there.

*(One of the waiters that came out before is coming out
to take their orders. CHRIS is on a roll though, so
when he sees the waiter approach he snaps at him.)*

Not now, Jethro!

(The waiter spins away quickly.)

Okay, you called her from a payphone...so they can't
trace your cell...We should be fine. We've got to buy
the train tickets with cash, put different names on the
ticket. That should cover us. And we'll hide out in
New York. We'd better make it six or eight months,
though...Just to be safe.

AJ

(Smiling big.)

Look at you go, man. We've got a criminal
mastermind here.

CHRIS

(Noticing his smile.)

I'm just trying to make the best of this...This is not
funny. We have to get out of town fast!

*(AJ is smiling big, on the verge of laughing. CHRIS
finally catches on.)*

We have...We have to...We don't have to do
anything, do we?

(AJ shakes his head.)

This whole thing...This whole death thing...It's all...

(AJ nods his head.)

183

You…You piece of shit.

AJ

(After letting out a big laugh, he mocks his panic and solemnity from earlier.)

Oh, Chris, what can we do? Oh my God, she's dead! She's dead!

(He laughs again.)

CHRIS

(Getting up from the booth and trying to strangle AJ.)

I can't believe you! I was…You had me…What the hell is your problem? You joke about death? You make jokes about murder? There was nothing funny about this! I was freaking out over here! You had me running from the cops, hiding out in another city…

AJ

(Still laughing.)

A regular Richard Kimble.

CHRIS

So…What? Why were you there all night?

AJ

What do you think? We had sex.

(CHRIS slumps back down after this.)

I saw your car when I left in the morning, I knew you were watching. I had a feeling you couldn't let go, and I was right.

CHRIS

This is not funny, shit head. You sleep with a girl I just told I had deep feelings for, and you do so right after you convince me not to see her again! I did just what you said. That night at the diner, I did my part. I did just what you said. I called Tina and had prostitute sex, and the next day you're counting ceiling tiles with the girl you told me to stay away from. Where's the loyalty? What happened to scruples?

AJ

Hey, at least I didn't make her put on her dance team uniform, man. You really thought I'd do that?

CHRIS

So, how'd it happen?

AJ

Well, I told her I was there to collect for you, and she was a little upset, but I told her you'd been sent to California for Rose Bowl preparation. Then I used the dead uncle routine.

CHRIS

You used the dead uncle thing. The story where you're real broken up about the recent death of your uncle, she's got to console you, and...You used a cheap line?

AJ

And boy, did she fall for it. Can't hold her liquor, though. Three glasses of wine and she was consoling the hell out of me. And don't bring that loyalty shit in here, because this might have been the most loyal thing a friend can do.

CHRIS

What?

AJ

Think about it, when wives cheat on their husbands, sometimes it is with a total stranger, and he never finds out. But, if his friend is the guy she sleeps with, that friend can tell the husband that his wife is a dirty whore, and therefore, the husband can take the wife to the cleaners in the divorce. Since Angela slept with a guy like me, you know she's got definite issues. And the fact that she would fall for such an obvious line is just pathetic. You can't have any respect for a woman like that.

CHRIS

But...

AJ

And we're missing the big picture here, my boy. Forget the sex. The fact that you followed me to her place is simple enough evidence to show that my convincing back at the diner didn't take. Sure, I know

185

you called Tina that night, but she told me what happened. I called her the next day and she said all you did was talk about our conversation, and about how much you'd like to be with Angela. I needed to be sure you were going to stick to our deal. When I saw your car outside her place, I had to know where your true interest lied. I spent all day thinking up that "Angela's dead" story. And it worked.

CHRIS

It worked if your goal was for me to want to choke you to death. You can't joke about murder, AJ. Not about real life murder.

AJ

Listen. When I told you that I'd killed that girl…that she was dead…You weren't all weepy and blubbering, "Oh, Angela. Oh, my darling Angela." Your main concern was my well-being, and how we were going to get out of here, and did we cover our tracks…You weren't mad at me, you didn't judge or blame me. You were focused on getting the hell out of Dodge. You should've seen yourself. It was like watching Moriarty plotting his next scheme. You reacted with complete and total regard for my safety, even when it meant running from the law. Even when the crime involved the accidental death of someone you cared about.

(He leans back in the booth.)

You know what I think…

CHRIS

Don't say it.

AJ

(In a childish voice.)

I think you love me. I think you love me.

CHRIS

(Starting to laugh)

Shut up. I'm serious. This is not funny.

(AJ gets up and starts poking at CHRIS.)

186

AJ

(Still singing.)

Christopher loves me. Christopher loves me.

CHRIS

(He succumbs in laughter, but he's still a little upset.)

Alright, alright! You proved your point. It doesn't change the fact that you had sex with the girl that was rightfully mine in the first place. I had first dibs. Maybe I could've used the dead uncle story, did you ever think of that?

AJ

You would've messed it up. You never do that scam right.

CHRIS

Yeah, you're probably right. So how was she, anyway? One to ten.

AJ

Maybe a six. Brunettes never really do it for me, you know that. But she had a waterbed.

CHRIS

Really?

AJ

Yeah, and that was cool. So, you really think we could've pulled it off? Running from "The Man."

CHRIS

It would've been nice to be notorious for a while. Always looking over our shoulder, jumping every time we heard a siren. Exciting times.

AJ

And you wouldn't have turned me in?

CHRIS

No…Well, not unless it was a really, really good reward. At least ten grand.

AJ

What a pal!

(He gets up.)

Let's get out of here, eh? Use your certificate some other time. Let's hit up the diner. We'll see Amy and Arch. They're going to love this story. What do you say?

CHRIS
(He gets up to leave as well.)
Sure, I don't really have a certificate anyway. I knew this place was non-smoking. I just wanted to throw you off your game.

AJ
Oh. That's right, the whole "Starsky/Hutch" thing.

CHRIS
Yeah. Once again, a plan that didn't work. You know, given the track record of my plans in the past, it's probably a good thing I didn't have to plan our daring escape to New York. We'd have been arrested before we hit Virginia.
(The Rolling Stone's "You Can't Always Get What You Want," begins low in the background.)

AJ
But what a story for Cell Block E, eh?

CHRIS
Yeah.

AJ
You know something good that will come out of this?

CHRIS
What?

AJ
(He lights a cigarette as he is about to leave. The hostess, CINDY LOU, starts to approach him to tell him to put it out, but he stops her with his finger as he takes a few puffs. She leaves him alone. As he puts his jacket over his arm, his wallet falls out of the inside pocket and onto the floor.)
If you were to ever come to doubt our friendship, I can always say, "Remember the Alamo."

*(They exit. "You Can't Always Get What You Want"
plays louder. LESLIE comes back on stage and wipes
down the table. She sees the wallet on the floor, picks it
up, looks at the driver's license, looks at the exit, then
looks through the money part, takes out the bills and
then throws the wallet in the garbage can near the
entrance.)*
LESLIE
(To herself and to the audience.)
Mega Superstar!
*(She puts the money in her pocket. Then walks off the
stage.)*

END SCENE 2
END ACT TWO
CURTAIN

Jeremey W. Gingrich

The Crisis of the Best Man

A Play in Two Acts

Jeremey W. Gingrich

The Crisis of the Best Man

A Play in Two Acts

This is the story of a good friend, Tommy Maloney, who is driving from Denver, Colorado to Fort Worth, Texas to be Best Man at his best friend's wedding. His friend is also his current roommate, but they could not go down together, because Reggie Green, the groom-to-be, had to go down earlier in the week for various obligations regarding the ceremony. As Tommy is driving down through the desolate state of Texas, he makes stops at various towns to get various things, and his emotions have the stability of a Duncan Yo-Yo. He is indecisive as to whether or not he is happy about his friend's marriage. The bride-to-be is Madeline James, and though Tommy knows her and has come to sort of like her, what does any man really know about any woman? Her father is a relatively good man, Frank James, proud of his baby girl, and more than willing to shell out for a big, expensive wedding. This is the story of the trip that brought them all together.

Time: The Present

Synopsis of Scenes

Act One—The Arrival

Scene 1—Pueblo, CO—Barnes & Noble Bookstore

Scene 2—Des Moines, NM—McDonald's Fast Food Restaurant

Scene 3—Flower Mound, TX—Gas Station

Scene 4—Fort Worth, TX—The Rehearsal Dinner

Act Two—The Escape

Scene 1—Fort Worth, TX—Groom's Room at the Church

Scene 2—Decatur, TX—McDonald's Fast Food Restaurant

Scene 3—Goodnight, TX—Ray's Truck Stop

As each scene takes us to a new city, an announcement will be made to the audience as to what city they are in. Something as simple as a sign that says the name of the city. There should be a big map of the trip stage right or stage left, one that is always there, and that can have a little toy car on it that is moved down along the path of the trip with each new scene.

Act One

Scene 1—*Pueblo, CO*—*This scene takes place in a bookstore. TOMMY is inside looking for a book on CD to play while he is on the road. It is a big bookstore, like a Barnes & Noble with a bunch of people in it, reading or writing or whatever. The sales clerk that comes to help him is an older man, HARRY...relatively eager to show off his knowledge of books. Other people sitting around are a college aged kid, JACK, and a middle-aged woman, CANDACE. JACK is doing homework, while CANDACE is writing down recipes from a cookbook. TOMMY is looking through* To Kill a Mockingbird. *He is reading the back of the book on CD. He is standing in front of the aisle that reads Audio Books and there is a small table to the left where JACK is working on something for school. To the right is another table where CANDACE is working on her cookbook. These two stay quiet until they come into play.*

HARRY
(Approaching TOMMY)

To Kill a Mockingbird? Let me guess...you loved the movie, right?

TOMMY
(Looking up)

Yeah.

HARRY

One of the classics. Gregory Peck was an icon for the ages after that role.

TOMMY

I actually just saw the movie for the first time. Everybody has always told me how great it was for all this time so I finally rented it, and the next day I bought it. The whole time I was watching, all I could think of was how great it must've been to have Atticus Finch for a father...you know. Such a presence...Now I wanted to check out the book.

195

HARRY

If you get the unabridged version you'll be introduced
to some characters that weren't used in the movie. But
if you like books turned into movies, you ought to
check out the Tolkien books...The Lord of the Rings
trilogy. The first movie almost won best picture, and
the books are...

TOMMY
(Chuckling)

No thanks, sir. I'm sure they're great books but I don't
want to end up like those "Lord of the Rings" book
geeks that come out of the movie theater saying stuff
like,

(Geeky voice)

"I can't believe they left out the scene where the orcs
find the crystal of hope..." or stuff like that. Besides,
though the movie was pretty good, I think the books
were made for those people who spent their high
school years playing Dungeons & Dragons.

JACK
(Looking up as that's said)

And what's wrong with that?

TOMMY
(Laughing at his faux pa)

Oh, sorry, man. Didn't mean to...

JACK

Those games teach strategy and foster creativity and
imagination.

TOMMY

And I bet you guys get all the girls.

JACK

I'll save the arguments in support of my hobbies for
someone who can read, Audio Book boy.

TOMMY

That's Audio Book Man to you, junior. And relax for
Christ's sake. All right, we've established we have
different tastes...let's move on. You're scaring...

(He looks at HARRY's nametag)
...Harry here. He's about to call bookstore security.
And besides, I happen to have a legitimate excuse for
looking for a book on CD. Granted, I've never been
the type to just sit somewhere and actually read
anything, unless I'm in the bathroom, but in this case I
have a long drive in front of me and I figure I'd do
something intellectual with my time on the road
instead of just a musical tour of my CD collection.
                    HARRY
Where you headed, I can probably recommend a book
that's as long as the trip. You look like you might be
Vegas bound.
                    TOMMY
Sadly, no. I'm headin' South...Texas. I got a wedding
in Fort Worth.
                    HARRY
Starting from here?
                    TOMMY
No. I headed out from Denver a couple hours ago. I
didn't make the decision to get a book for the road
until I was past Colorado Springs.
                    HARRY
Well, you've got about ten to twelve hours left in front
of you...give or take some traffic problems.
        (He looks through the aisle)
                    JACK
Who's getting married?
                    TOMMY
My friend Reggie. He's my roommate up in Denver,
and he's marrying this chick who insisted on a Texas
wedding.
                    JACK
Everything's bigger in Texas.

HARRY

Aha! Perfect! An essential. The Adventures of
Huckleberry Finn. Unabridged. Ten hours. It'll wrap
up right as you drive into Fort Worth.

TOMMY

You know, I've always wanted to read that. It was
assigned in school but it was always more fun to not
read the book and bullshit the essay. That's how I
would foster creativity and imagination. I got the gist
just from cultural osmosis...Rebellious boy, runaway
slave, a raft on the Mississippi.

HARRY

It's so much more, though. There are little events that
happen to them on the way which make the book itself
almost a collection of short stories tied together by the
river. Mark Twain was immortalized in American
literature with this one piece of work.

(Hands the discs to TOMMY)

TOMMY

You talked me into it.

(Looking at the back of the discs)

Hey and look, Michael Caine is the narrator. If nothing
else, it'll be amusing hearing a British actor doing a
Southern accent.

JACK

Let me get this straight. Your roommate is getting
married?

TOMMY

Yeah.

JACK

He didn't live with her first?

TOMMY

He wanted to, but you know, she was in college in her
own hometown...It made more sense for her to live
with her folks and finish her degree. Now that she's
finished, she just graduated in June, they're getting
married.

JACK
Have they known each other long?
CANDACE
I'm sorry, but what business is that of yours.
(To TOMMY)
You come in here to buy a book for the road and out of
nowhere some kid is asking you twenty questions
about the love life of your good friend. I just hate nosy
people!

JACK
(Taken aback by the outburst)
I'm sorry, jeez. I was just curious as to the process,
that's all. A few of my friends got married right out of
high school and it's made their lives a lot harder. I'm
sure they knew that going in, so I just wanted to know
what leads people...

TOMMY
Relax, uh...
(Snapping his fingers to get a name)
JACK
Jack.

TOMMY
Relax, Jack, you don't have to explain yourself to me.
(To CANDACE)
This is my vision of what society should
be...Complete strangers sharing intimate details of
their lives in random settings. We're all weird people,
and we do weird things for weird reasons. But through
exploration of those reasons, we get a more intimate
portrait of the people we meet...kind of makes us more
like a family.

CANDACE
You read Hillary Clinton's <u>It Takes a Village</u>, didn't
you?

TOMMY
For instance, I wonder why you would sit here in this
bookstore copying recipes out of a cookbook, when

you could just, you know, buy the cookbook, which is what I'm sure Harry here would love for you to do, and would kind of be one of the defining differences between this place and…say…a library.

CANDACE

What?

JACK
(Still to TOMMY)

The thing is, women come to bookstores like this because it's seen as a good place to meet intellectual men, men who value books and reading and pursuits of an intellectual nature. Think about it, it sure beats the hell out of the lunkheads they're going to meet in a bar or club, right? You go to those places to find sex. You come to places like this for a husband. And so these women sit down and copy a bunch of recipes from cookbooks until finally the man of their dreams comes up thinking, "Here's a woman who likes to cook." And then they strike up a conversation.

CANDACE

This is so offensive it makes me want to vomit.

JACK
(Pointing to the other books on the table by CANDACE)

And sometimes they put other books on the table to show a variety of interests, so the unwitting admirer also thinks, "Wow, she's really diverse." What else have you got there? Ethan Frome and The Autobiography of Malcolm X…Hmm. It was an article in Cosmo.

TOMMY

Is this true?

(She ignores them)

Come on, miss, the community thing doesn't work if
one of us is withholding. Share.

CANDACE
(Succumbing, after a while)
It's Candace, not Miss. And he wasn't supposed to
have read that article in Cosmo.

JACK
What can I say; I'm a sensitive guy.

TOMMY
And I'm sure it has nothing to do with all the sex
articles they put in there too, right?

JACK
Anyway, back to my original question, before we
started playing "The Dating Game," have your friend
and his fiancé' known each other long?

TOMMY
They've been seeing each other for eight months now.
That seems like enough time to get to know a person,
doesn't it?

CANDACE
Who can say?

JACK
I just thought it was the common practice these days to
live together before getting married. Kind of like test-
driving a car before buying it.

TOMMY
I thought that analogy was made to refer to having sex
before marriage? And they have.

CANDACE
Jesus, we got a couple of hopeless romantics here. I'm
getting weepy.

TOMMY
(To both of them)
But you're thinking so much could be revealed in
living together that it could unearth serious problems?

JACK

People have strange living habits, and they hide them during the dating process…especially women. Men are guilty of their fair share, but all the phony shit women do to get a man, once that goes away most men are blindsided. It comes in a variety of forms. Nagging is a key form, but even just natural living conditions can be a source of discontent, making a woman an almost unbearable living partner. Candace you can vouch for this.

CANDACE

I haven't wanted to punch someone in the face this badly for some time now.

HARRY

(As HARRY walks back over with another customer, a roughly high school age girl TRACY)

And here you are, Miss. The books on tape and CD. The classics are…

TOMMY

Harry! You seem like an older man, no offense, but weathered by the tribulations of time, and I see you have a wedding band on. Can you help us out on this?

HARRY

Well, I'd rather not…

TOMMY

(To TRACY, who eavesdrops as she pretends to shop for an audio book)

Excuse us.

(He pulls HARRY away)

How long have you been married, Harry?

HARRY

Actually, I was married for 37 years, but my wife passed away less than a month ago. She had got the cancer, and died on a Tuesday…

TOMMY

(Quick and dismissive of his grief.)

Yeah, yeah. We're all real sorry and your loss is great
and oh the mystery of life…But when she was alive,
what made the marriage last for 37 years? I guess I
mean to say, weren't there any times when you would
just be the proverbial fox, willing to gnaw his own leg
off to escape the trap? Or was it all just peaches and
cream?

JACK

Don't you mean the proverbial peaches and cream?
(Shaking his head)
I hate when people use the term "the proverbial."
Everyone knows it's a proverb! Just say it!

CANDACE
(To JACK)

I use it quite a bit. It's a phrase people say when they
are making a point. It adds emphasis to the analogy
and helps the flow of the conversation.

JACK

How does adding that to the conversation help the
flow? It's a big word for the sake of saying a big…

TRACY
(Turning violently)

Jesus Christ! The man's wife is dead!! What the hell is
the matter with you people?
(She throws her book on the counter and storms off.)

HARRY

No, no. It's alright. They say it's good to talk about
these things…I guess you people are as good as
anybody else. When Babs and I got married we were
fresh out of high school, because that's what happened
in the town I came from…High school sweethearts got
married. And we immediately slipped into the pattern
we had observed from our parents, I went to work all
day, she stayed home, we had some kids…I'm not
really sure what you're looking for.

203

TOMMY

What about all the stuff that they say about nagging? I saw my mother do it from time to time, but was too young to appreciate its effects. Did that "leaving the toilet seat up" sort of thing ever happen with you?

CANDACE

In defense of the female gender, that is a terrible inconvenience.

JACK

Oh, please! Just look before you leap, problem solved.

HARRY

Sure it happened once or twice, but a marriage is so much bigger than that. Petty inconveniences and little stuff like that isn't...

JACK

It's supposed to be bigger than that, but that's what the marriage becomes all about.

CANDACE

And what the hell do you know? What are you? 20? Maybe 21?

JACK

I have an easy recollection of my parents, who divorced my senior year of high school. The thing I remember most are the asinine arguments about such little, petty things. Something as stupid as putting a coat on the back of a chair instead of the closet could become Ali/Frasier right at the dinner table. And I'm 21, not that that adds or subtracts from the meaning of my message and that is this: "Marriage is a woman's attempt to make a man obey her every wish, both spoken and unspoken." And anything less is something to bitch about.

CANDACE
(Looking at him slyly)
There's a lot of anger in this one. Estrogen-targeted frustration.

TOMMY
Putting that obvious observation aside, he does have a
point. Often you do hear about marriages becoming
continuous shouting matches. I think almost every
married man I've met, married longer than 5 years,
believes matrimony to be an institution of sheer
volume, rather than emotion. And I'm scared…Scared
for my friend Reggie, because I don't want him to have
to go through that. His voice has a tendency to become
high pitched when he shouts. It's not very intimidating.
And, worse case, what if the whole thing fails?
CANDACE
Divorce is a difficult thing.
TOMMY
Difficult? That can't begin to describe it. This is a
person you've decided to spend the rest of your life
with, and then, after one or two…or five or ten years of
bickering and unhappiness, even possible infidelity,
you come to the mutual, and sometimes not mutual,
agreement that you should never be in the same room
together ever again. Jesus, why is he getting married?
*(He sits down, exhausted by the thought, holding his
head.)*
HARRY
Relax, sir. It really isn't all that bad. I won't tell you its
all days of wine and roses, but sharing your life with
another person, your whole life, is a feeling that can't
be described by stories or recollections. The years I
was married to Barbara were the best years of my
life…And when I think of the times we had, even the
so-called "bad times," I realize I wouldn't trade them
for anything in the world.
*(CANDACE is visibly effected by the story, but after
thinking, she solemnly says.)*
CANDACE
I cheated on my ex-husband.

JACK

Your ex-hus…You did what?

CANDACE

(To JACK)

You don't get to say anything here!

(To HARRY)

George and I had been married for only three years, and the guy was just somebody who picked me up at a bar. I was out with my girlfriends and this guy just started hitting on me, compliments, saying how sexy I was. That hadn't happened to me in so long…He was just some young guy, about 20, who picked me up at a bar. And I could never say my husband hit me, or neglected me, or cheated on me himself…I just wanted to have casual sex with this young kid. George was a good man. He worked long hours at a job he hated to make our lives very comfortable, and the guilt I felt after my infidelity was sickening. So, after wrestling with the decision for a while, I told him…

(Pause)

…to ease my guilt. In one sentence, in one selfish moment, I ruined the man I promised to share the rest of my life with. The look on his face made me want to die. He served me the papers two weeks later. Now, when I think of the good times my husband and I had, I thank God that it lasted as long as it did. But I know I would trade all the good times, all my good fortune, if I could just take back that feeling I inflicted on the man I loved. No, Harry, marriage is not all days of wine and roses.

TOMMY

(After a pause)

I couldn't let…if anything like that happened to Reggie…

HARRY

It doesn't happen to everybody. But you are right, if it happened to me when I was married, I would have lost my mind. The trust factor in a marriage...

JACK

And how could you know, for sure, it didn't happen to you while you were married?

TOMMY

Hey, now...

CANDACE

Jesus Christ!

JACK

Hey, I can appreciate your honesty in this particular dream society we've created here, but if we are going to play the honesty game let's explore all avenues. For every guilty wife who confesses her sins to her husband, or every jealous hubby who walks in on the act between his woman and the mailman...or the plumber...or...

HARRY

I'm going to help other customers now.

(Turns to leave.)

JACK

No wait...

TOMMY

No, let him go. I also want to get down to the honest answers about marriage and what not...But let the man be. He's got a lot on his mind at this moment. And I think I've heard all I'd care to hear today.

(To CANDACE)

I also really appreciate your participation in my little social experiment here, Candace. You and Jack and Harry have been great at getting my brain working at this initial part of my trek down to Texas. I understand your mission here...

(He picks up her recipe book)

...and I'm pretty sure I'm gonna start reading Cosmo myself, but I hope your objective of finding a new husband fails...No offense. Marriage is the last thing I would wish on anybody looking for happiness. Now, I'm gonna ride through the barren state of Texas and let Michael Caine tell me the story of a boy and his raft...and try to think of some way to keep my friend from going anywhere near a wedding chapel. Wish me luck, and you take care.

(He exits)

(They wave goodbye and then after a pause.)

JACK

You think he can do it?

CANDACE

I don't know, but it's gonna be a hard conversation, either way.

(Starts writing again.)

Oh, and by the way I fucking hate you.

JACK

Careful, people will say we're in love.

END SCENE 1

SCENE 2—*Des Moines, NM. Fast Food restaurant. This is a fast food restaurant not unlike McDonald's, in fact it is McDonald's. There is a counter from which to order, a menu up at the top, above the counter, and tables strewn about the set. There is even a side counter for condiments. There are doors stage right that act as the principal entrance and exit. There are six people waiting for food in line. One is dressed in hunting camouflage, MARCUS, another is a mother who is constantly yelling at her kids who are off-stage, playing in the Play Place. Two people are dressed regularly and play no part in the drama of the scene, they just order their food and leave. The two other ones are random people, dressed relatively respectfully, two friends. The two friends, JAY and DAVE, are at the*

208

front of the line, while the woman, CLARICE, is upstage yelling at her kids.

CLARICE
(Yelling offstage)

Billy! Stop pulling your brother's hair! I swear to God if I have to come out there...Tommy! Stop crying! You stop that crying! That's what you get for letting him pull on your hair! Just let me get the food and you can kill each other back home!

(She walks back into line, but JAY and DAVE are in front of her but behind two other random people. Upon hearing her yelling, they motion for her to go to the front of the line. She replies with the most gentle of voices.)

Oh, thank you.

(She then speaks softly to the person taking orders at the counter.)

(TOMMY comes in through the doors after a while, pacing like a crazy person. He has out his cell phone but he is not talking on it. He is mumbling to himself and he walks back outside but then comes back in and is still mumbling.)

TOMMY

Should I...? What would I say? I have to...but what if?

(CLARICE has ordered her food and has moved aside to wait for her order but while TOMMY is wrestling with himself, she yells back upstage.)

CLARICE

Tommy! You stop that crying!

(TOMMY jumps as she yells)
TOMMY
(Thinking she's talking to him)

I'm not crying. I'm just upset about...

(Noticing he doesn't know her)

I'm sorry, were you shrieking at me?

209

CLARICE

No, my kids. Had to have Happy Meals. Had to play in
the Fun Place. You know, I can remember doing this
as a kid, but I don't remember needing Quaaludes to…
(Yelling at the kids again)
…act like a civilized person!

JAY

They had Play Places at McDonald's when you were a
kid?

(DAVE cringes at the question.)

CLARICE

Just how old do you think I am?
*(While this exchange is going on, TOMMY is still
wrestling his demons.)*

DAVE

Quick, change the subject.

JAY

(To them both.)
You remember when they use to have Mayor
McCheese in commercials when we were kids? God, I
use to love that guy.

DAVE

That was the guy with the big hamburger head dressed
in that official looking uniform, right? Whatever
happened to him? Do they even use him anymore?

JAY

I think he was impeached after a big scandal.
Suspicious ties to the Hamburglar.
*(CLARICE sees her food is ready so she gives the boys
a dirty look and tends to her food. The two guys just
glance at each other in relief. She leaves her purse on
the floor, no one notices.)*

CLARICE

*(Holding the happy meals and McDonalds bag. Yelling
at the direction of the PlayPlace.)*
Alright, damn it. I got your food now let's get the hell
out of here! I'm not coming out there!

(She exits.)
(TOMMY is now just standing and thinking. The two random people are now being taken care of, while JAY and DAVE and MARCUS are still waiting in line.)

MARCUS
(To TOMMY, in a Southern accent)
What you got to be upset about?

TOMMY
I'm sorry?

MARCUS
You said you were a little upset. Most analysts say it's better to talk about it. They say the release is therapeutic.
(TOMMY looks his outfit up and down.)

TOMMY
And are you an analyst yourself?

MARCUS
No, not an analyst by trade. But I like to think we all possess a certain healing power from time to time. And what's a better place to look for a quick fix than a fast food place?

TOMMY
(Reluctant)
I'm...I'm debating whether or not to call my best friend and tell him my reservations about his wedding?

MARCUS
Well, if you need to make a reservation you should probably call him and make them. I don't see where the debate comes in?

TOMMY
No, not make reservations! I have reservations! I don't think he's making a good decision! I hate the fact that he's willing to throw his life away! That's having a reservation!

JAY
(Eavesdropping)

A reservation is also a designated plot of land for
Native Americans. Let's not forget that.

DAVE

Would you quit it, please? The man obviously has an
issue here. Try to be helpful.

MARCUS

Well, now that I got the situation straight...

TOMMY

You'll excuse me if your opinion doesn't hold a lot of
weight with me at this point.

MARCUS

You'd think that would keep me from talking, but...If
this man really is your best friend, he's going to value
your opinion whether he agrees with it or not. He's
kept you around over the years for some reason, so
he'll probably be thankful and take your advice under
consideration.

JAY

*(Laughing at the suggestion, saying this kind of under
his breath)*

Ha! What planet is this guy from?

TOMMY

And your two cents...?

JAY

(They are at the front of the line now)

Dave, you go ahead.

*(Motioning for DAVE to order. DAVE orders. Back to
TOMMY)*

This guy, your friend...

TOMMY

Reggie.

JAY

Reggie thinks he has found the woman he is going to
spend the rest of his life with, right? This is the woman
he wants to bear his children, to grow old with and to
die with and you want to tell him he's making a
mistake?

TOMMY

No good?

DAVE
(Motioning for JAY to order)

You're up, man.

JAY

Just a second.

(Back to TOMMY)

One of two things will happen. Either he says, "Oh, yeah, you're right." And he tells the woman that he's not ready for marriage...how many days till the wedding?

TOMMY

Three.

JAY
(To DAVE, who's been pulling)

Just order for me.

(Back to TOMMY)

Okay, so this guy tells the woman he doesn't want to marry her three days before the wedding so she, of course, leaves him after a huge crying fit and, more than likely, some physical abuse. And after surviving his thrashing, maybe his happiness lasts a few years...and then the demons come. He then starts to wonder why he's still alone after all these years, and how instead of nursing a glass of whiskey he might be watching his son's Little League Games at this point in his life if he hadn't listened to you, his best friend. And with that thought comes a bitterness you cannot possibly fathom.

TOMMY

Okay, I don't like that scenario. What's behind door number two?

JAY

Door number two has your best friend disregarding your advice, and marrying this woman anyway. Now there's this uncomfortable thing out there that prevents

213

the three of you from having a good relationship. Pretty soon, you're spending less time with your friend because of this uncomfortable thing out there. Then, he starts spending time with either his supportive friends, friends who like his wife and think he made the right decision, or he gets married friends and they do couple things together. Before you know it, you're getting a phone call at Thanksgiving and a card at Christmas, and all you can do is hum a few bars of "The Way We Were."

DAVE

(To TOMMY)

He paints a pretty picture, don't he?

JAY

(Turns around and sees that his food has been brought to him.)

What is this? I can't eat this.

DAVE

(Taking the tray to a table, still on stage.)

You'll eat it and you'll like it.

TOMMY

(Following them to their table.)

Are you telling me there is nothing I can do here that can work out in a positive way? I have concerns here. Concerns concerning my best friend's life, for God's sake.

DAVE

Well, have you thought about deception?

TOMMY

What?

DAVE

What I do, when I have to tell someone something important that might have negative ramifications, is I mask it as a story. Say, I'm in your situation. Instead of telling this friend…this Reggie…about my reservations as to his new bride, I would tell him that I heard about a guy who got married and that it didn't turn out too well. There would be some details you'd have to work in there, of course…You know, make the story a little more personal.

JAY

You do that to avoid confrontation. It's a real chicken shit way of handling conflict, I'll tell you that.

MARCUS

(Walking past their table with a tray of his food.)
You know that actually sounds like a good idea. That way, your opinion gets out there, without really being seen as your opinion. You've given him pause, and in that time he will reconsider the concept of marriage. This does not mean that he will change his mind altogether mind you, but maybe the moment of clarity will allow him to make a decision based on his brain, rather than any other organ that may be doing the thinking.

TOMMY

(Fed up with MARCUS.)
Are you still here?

(MARCUS is upset. So he picks up his tray and heads off.)

DAVE

Aren't we all giving marriage a bad rap right off the bat here? Let's keep in mind some pretty good things have come from marriage. I count myself as one of them. I'd be willing to bet that most of us here were born in wedlock, and raised that way as well. Kids are a great thing that two married people share with one another.

(CLARICE storms back into the McD's and grabs her purse from the floor.)

CLARICE

(To the people in the place)
Nobody could run this out to me before I got two miles down the road?!

DAVE, JAY, TOMMY, MARCUS

Sorry.

CLARICE
(Looking out to the car.)

Alright, you bastards, get back in the car! Billy, stop putting things into the tailpipe! Jesus!
(She leaves again obviously frustrated.)
TOMMY
(To DAVE)

You were saying?

DAVE

Well, how was the parental situation when you were growing up? Did your parents get along, or what?

TOMMY

Well, they got along, but they didn't seem happy. I mean, when I'm around my friends, I'm happy. I'm not pretending. And I can tell, with them, it was almost like they were tolerating each other's company rather than enjoying it. And hey, they're still married to this day.

JAY

There you go, at least they stayed together.

TOMMY

Yeah, but that was their second marriage, they had both been married before and, from what I've heard, they ended badly.

JAY

So maybe this is good for your friend…you know…get that first marriage out of the way.

TOMMY

What, like a throw away marriage?

JAY

Exactly. When the priest gives the vows, he can talk in less definitive terms. Instead of "as long as you both shall live," it can be "until you've just had enough."

216

TOMMY

Jesus, you really know how to tug the heartstrings.
You should write greeting cards.

JAY

So, what's the story with this friend of yours? He isn't
marrying his high school sweetheart, is he?

DAVE

Oh, would you stop, please.

JAY

I will not stop. You still owe me for that, you know. I
saved your life, my friend.

DAVE

(Noticing TOMMY's confusion.)

I mentioned once, only once, back in high school that
it would have been…that I might've married the girl I
was seeing at the time.

(To JAY)

And no, I did not propose, and no, I did not buy her a
ring. But for some reason, Jay always thinks I was
renting a tuxedo and two steps away from the altar.

JAY

I could see it in your face, man.

DAVE

Okay, maybe I did do a little bit of planning. And I
was, sort of, writing out the speech for when I would
have asked for her father's permission…

TOMMY

You were writing out a speech for that?

DAVE

Well, I wanted it to be perfect, you know? I wouldn't
want to come out all flustered and stuttering.

TOMMY

But if it seems rehearsed I'd think…

JAY

The point here is…if you'll allow me…That could
have been it for you. You think we'd be sitting here
now? No! You'd be off changing a diaper and I'd

217

be…well, we wouldn't be here together, I'll tell you that.

TOMMY

So what happened?

DAVE

Well, Jay was with the basketball team on one of their away games…

TOMMY

You played ball?

JAY

Mascot.

DAVE

…And on this trip it turns out that Steph, that was the girl's name, she was a cheerleader at the time…

TOMMY

I've never been with a cheerleader.

DAVE

Oh, they earn their reputation, friend. Anyway, it turns out that Steph decided to celebrate the road win with one of the players after the game…

TOMMY

Ouch.

DAVE

…Actually with several players after the game.

TOMMY

Double Ouch. You were right, they do earn their reputation. Jeez, you must have been pissed.

DAVE

I was for a while, but the team took States that year, so…

JAY

You see, if I wasn't lookin' out for him, that kind of stuff would have eaten him up if they were married. That's the main problem with high school sweethearts getting married. Older people can say to themselves, "Okay, I'm not really attractive anymore, this is the best I can do." How can you be expected to make a decision like that right out of high school, when you've got so many attractive years left ahead of you. The day after the nuptials you might run into the Swedish bikini team and you'd always be thinking, "Could I get her? Could I get her? Could I get those three?" It's hard enough finding out what college to go to, let alone deciding on the one person you're going to spend your whole damn life with. And sure, high school sweetheart stuff is sweet. They're in love. Love is great! People write songs about it. But if you've only been with one woman from age 17 for the whole rest of your life…that takes more than love.

DAVE

That's why high school sweetheart stories are the most romantic. Because they're the most challenging. Look at the Huxtables…

TOMMY

That's the problem with being raised on television. "The Cosby Show" family only stayed together for nine seasons, but we use them as a representation for long-lasting romance.

(Thinking)

But I always liked the episodes when they'd dance at the end. Remember?

(Nostalgically)

They'd play that slow jazz…

JAY

Fuck the Huxtables, that's the type of bullshit propaganda marriage has going for it. We get "happily ever after," and concepts of monogamy crammed down our throat when we're kids. Which is a contradiction to our nature, discovered at puberty, which is to be with as many women as we can? When people get married their mind and their eyes still wander, it's just a matter of time and inclination as to when the body follows. The perfect marriage is a fantasy held by almost everyone, and fidelity is the

dream behind that fantasy…and that's just what it
is…a dream. And people don't change just because
they got a ring on their finger.
DAVE
Speakin' of which, if you can talk your friend out of
this marriage deal, there's gonna be a big ordeal…you
know…with the bride all upset and her family
upset…basically a lot of people upset at this poor
guy…What was his name again?
TOMMY
Reggie.
DAVE
Yeah, Reggie's not gonna have a real good day if he
doesn't go through with the nuptials. But when all is
said and done, he would probably want to get the ring
back from her, wouldn't he? That's got to be a hard
question to ask, no matter how much time passes. I
mean, how big was it?
TOMMY
Two-carat diamond with platinum band.
*(JAY and DAVE react with the appropriate
astonishment.)*
JAY
Two carats is a lot of lettuce.
(Makes the "Money" hand motion.)
TOMMY
Good place to start a marriage, isn't it? The poor
house.
JAY
Oh, jeez, add financial problems into the mix and
that's when the real problems start to surface. Lack of
money is a catalyst for all unhappiness in marriage.
DAVE
Listen to yourself! Are you listening to yourself? All of
us, Jesus…What the hell do we know? God, we sit
here, and the first thing we say is how you should tell
your friend to drop this girl. That's the first thing that

pops into our heads. Then we bounce around, "Oh, can you get the ring back." "Jeez, wasn't that Cosby Show a load of shit." Or, "The first marriage is the throw away marriage." Shit!! We sound like old men beaten down by a long life of twists and turns and none of us were born before the Goddamn Carter administration...

TOMMY

Come on. I don't think that this should be a reflection on Jimmy Carter...

DAVE

(Now anger is up.)

No, it's a reflection on how cynical we've allowed ourselves to become in such a small amount of time on this planet. We focus on the negative side of a thing before we even give a snowball's chance to the positive. If you simply have reservations about your friend marrying this woman, I would consider that a glass-half-empty view on marriage. But with the conversation we've just had here the past fifteen minutes I think we all took that glass and shattered it into a thousand fuckin' pieces. Marriage can be a wonderful thing, and love could be the greatest thing of all, just like they say in all those songs, but we'll never know because we're too busy tearing it down the second it shows its ugly face! We weren't always like this, I'm sure of it. We've had some positive thoughts haven't we? Think back. Remember that scene at the end of "The Natural?" With Robert Redford throwing the ball with his son in the field, Glenn Close looking on as the doting wife. Didn't you see yourself in that role when you saw that scene?

(Pause, as the boys look back in their mind's eye and smile.)

And Jesus, why did that bitch have to sleep with the whole fuckin' basketball team! I could be sharing my life with someone now! I should be playing catch with

221

my kids' right now, damn it! I had so many visions of where I would be at this point in my life and instead of the Rockwell painting I envisioned for myself, I'm in a fucking McDonald's having this conversation with you! Damn it! I need to splash some water on my face.

(He storms out.)

TOMMY

That's a lot of remorse for a guy to carry around all these years. I guess, even though he was young, he really thought he had found "The One." And it will forever be seen as "The One That Got Away."

JAY

Yeah, and just think how pissed he'll be if he ever finds out that whole "Sleeping with the basketball team" story was a big fuckin' lie.

TOMMY

What?

JAY

I couldn't let him marry that chick, man. She...if he'd have been with her...Look, I was right to do what I did, okay? I believed that then, and I believe that now. And even though she denied it, very vocally, he still believed me over her. Given that fact, I think he wanted to believe it, too. That's why, no matter what his rants happen to be years later, I still think you should do anything in your power to stop this wedding.

(DAVE comes back onstage.)

TOMMY

You alright?

DAVE

Yeah, just a spontaneous venting session. I'm sorry you had to witness that.

TOMMY

No, it's okay. It's good for me to hear these things...and they're emotional subjects, so it's inevitable that the emotions take over once in a while. And given the weight of the situation, and certain

222

elements that have come to my attention, I think it would be...obtrusive for me to say anything about Reggie's life at this stage. But I will always be there to support him, through the good times and the bad, and I will try to never think "What if this?" or "What if that?" But I can't guarantee anything. I have this affinity for bitching and complaining, so I wouldn't be surprised if a little of that came into play now and again. But I swear I will not be the one to break the peace.

JAY

It's your funeral.

TOMMY

No, it's his wedding.

DAVE

You getting any food, buddy?

TOMMY

No, I've lost my appetite. I'm just gonna hit the road. I'm about a third of the way through Michael Caine's telling of Huckleberry Finn. Thanks again for your time.

(He leaves. DAVE and JAY are still sitting there. JAY looks down at his tray, up at DAVE. DAVE can see something is on his mind.)

DAVE

What? What is it?

JAY
(Dismissive)

Nothing.

DAVE

No, no. You look like you got something on your mind. Spill it.

JAY

When...
(looks down at his food. Then switches tone totally)
When have you ever seen me order the Filet O Fish? Jesus, Dave, it's a square fish!

DAVE
Oh, don't start with this...I ordered what I thought
you...

END SCENE 2

SCENE 3—*Flower Mound, TX—The Gas Station. TOMMY is real close to his final destination now, but has stopped for gas before reaching Fort Worth. The set is the interior of the Gas Station, with coolers for sodas, a snack set up and various car stuff for sale, as well. There are two guys standing behind the counter, dressed as attendants. One is just a normal Joe, who I'll call JOE for now. But the other guy is a Mexican, who speaks and understands very little English, who is addressed as PACO. The scene opens with JOE and PACO talking behind the counter, and as JOE talks to him, he leads him around the store. TOMMY will enter shortly.*
JOE
Alright, Paco, I'm not sure what you've heard about our little store, but we're one of the luckier ones. Even when we work the late shifts, very rarely will anyone come in and hold up the place. Armed robbery is not the problem we have here. However, we do have an increasing problem with shoplifters. These are typically kids, or bums from the street, even grown men trying to recapture some of that youthful lawlessness. They waltz in here and stuff their pockets and I'm left looking like a chump. We've got the surveillance camera but all that does is tell me at the end of the day who stole from me, but they never come back and say, "Hey, I stole from you two weeks back so you should probably keep an eye on me." So that's what I've hired you for, Paco. You with me so far?
PACO
(Very slow, bad English, but a beaming smile.)
It is my first day.

JOE
(To himself, very sarcastic.)
God, I love Texas.
(Back to Paco. Leading him to where the front door
would be. Speaking very slowly.)
When a customer…walks into the store…
(He pauses a lot to make sure PACO understands what
he's saying, and he walks him through the entire
store.)
You…You follow…
(He motions to him, grabbing his arms. And keeping
him next to him.)
…follow man who come through door…every
man…walk right beside and watch.
(Uses his fingers to motion towards his eyes.)
Always watch.
(He then leads him back to the door.)
Follow?
(PACO looking somewhat confused, nods.)
JOE
We're coming along.
(He then walks back behind the counter.)
(TOMMY then walks into the place. He is nonchalant
and it seems as though he has come to terms with
REGGIE'S marriage.)
JOE
(To TOMMY)
Afternoon, sir.
TOMMY
Afternoon.
(He walks to the back of the store and looks in the
coolers for a drink. As he walks to the back JOE nods
to PACO and PACO starts to follow him very close
and watching his every move. TOMMY simply moves
about the store for a while and occasionally smiles at
PACO, who smiles back. After the sodas and browsing
the chips and peanuts section, TOMMY is perusing the

225

candy section, he picks up a selection, then says to PACO, somewhat awkwardly.)
I've loved this stuff since I was a kid…haven't seen it around for a long time.

PACO

(Very slow, bad English, but a beaming smile.)
It is my first day.

(They exchange awkward looks, then TOMMY moves back to the drink place and is looking at the selections.)

TOMMY

You all don't have Raspberry Iced Tea?

JOE

No. Just lemon.

(Looking out of what would be the front window of the Gas Station.)
Sir, is that your VW bug out on pump 4?

TOMMY

Yeah, but I paid at the pump, so you ain't gotta worry about it.

JOE

Oh, okay.

(To PACO.)
Paco, no follow. Back to door.

(PACO looks confused.)
No need to follow.

TOMMY

(Walking up to the counter with a soda and candy.)
You gotta have him follow people when they come in the store?

JOE

Yeah, sorry about that. Problems with kids and what not.

(TOMMY is now at the counter.)

TOMMY

And what makes you think I'm not a threat.

(He obviously and comically puts his soda and candy in his pockets.)
Oh, the car, right? Man driving a newer car is not as inclined to steal little bits of convenient store junk food?

JOE
Well, okay.

TOMMY
No? Then what...

JOE
Well, not for nothing and please take no offense, but a man in a yellow clown car doesn't seem very threatening to me.

TOMMY
Clown car, eh? What makes you think I'd take offense? Well, it's been called worse...

(Just then two older people come through the door into the store, MARGARET and GERALD. GERALD goes straight to the bathroom, and MARGARET follows him close, but they go slow. Slow enough for this huge argument to take shape. MARGARET starts it up as he walks in, and when they walk in and to the bathroom, PACO follows closely, but since they storm in, PACO has to jog a little to keep up.)

MARGARET
I can't believe you! You are disgusting! There's no way I'm letting you back in the car! You think I'm going to let you back in the car with me after this disgusting display you are mistaken! What were you, raised in a barn? This is not the behavior of a civilized man. And we still have people to meet! Oh my God, we cannot have dinner with Becky and Robert with you like this!

GERALD
(From the closed door of the bathroom.)
You didn't do the laundry! I'm just adjusting.

227

MARGARET

You're blaming me! I can't believe you!
(To PACO, who is standing close)
Can you believe this man!
(Back to the door.)
You said,
(mocking GERALD's voice)
"No, honey, you just take care of your clothes and I'll
wash my own." That's what you said! Now, here we
are, we have a nice dinner with the Harrison's in
Dallas, I'm wearing my Sunday dress and my good
shoes and you're wearing your Brooks Brothers suit
with Stacy Adams shoes and no underwear! And now
you're trying to say it's my fault?
(To PACO)
He's got some nerve!
(Thinking)
Heaven's, if they ever found out…
*(GERALD has flushed and washed his hands and
walks out of the bathroom and walks to where the
candy is.)*

GERALD

(Coming out of the bathroom drying his hands.)
You know what? I guarantee you Becky and Rob find
out I'm not wearing any underwear! I guarantee you!
You know why? Because that will be the first thing
you say to them! Not "Hello," not "Great to see you,"
the first thing out of your mouth will be "I'm so sorry
Gerald's not wearing any underwear." You know how
I know? Because you haven't shut up about it since we
left home! Forty-five minutes this has been going on!
Forty-five minutes of blah blah blah, and why? For
what? If you were so concerned, why didn't you do a
wash? This whole thing could be avoided…

MARGARET

You were the one that told me not to wash your
clothes! You said it made you feel bad, like I was

doing all the work and you weren't! I did what you asked me to do!
GERALD
Well, believe me, had I known that I would be entering the eighth concentric circle of hell over this damn laundry conflict, I would have never asked you not to do my wash! Besides, I've accepted the fact that I'm dining al fresco...so just relax and let it be! Ooh, there's the jerky.
MARGARET
(To PACO who is a little scared by standing right next to them.)
Do you mind! We're having a moment.
JOE
Paco, back to door.
(To TOMMY, who is mesmerized by the couple's conversation.)
I ought to get the kid a medal for lasting that long.
MARGARET
(GERALD is taking beef jerky back to the front counter.)
What are you doing? You're going to buy that?
GERALD
That's the general idea.
MARGARET
We're going to have dinner here in less than an hour! What are you thinking? You're going to spoil...
GERALD
I'm going to spoil my dinner?! Oh my God, the ghost of my mother appears to me in a convenient store! I've been craving something to nosh this whole drive and this is our first stop! So I get a little snack before dinner, I think the restaurant will forgive me!
MARGARET
(Snatches the bag from him, looking at it.)
Look at all the sodium in this! Your blood pressure is gonna skyrocket! Dr. Asher said to stay away from too much salt...

229

GERALD

Dr. Asher said for me to stay away from everything
that I enjoy! That's a diagnosis I can do without.

MARGARET

So, you just do whatever you want despite the advice
of trained professionals? You are the most stubborn
man on…

TOMMY
(TOMMY abruptly interrupts.)
OH MY GOD!!! Is this really how it is? Holy God!
Can you hear yourselves? Can you even hear
yourselves?

GERALD
(A little upset.)
Excuse me?

TOMMY
(Mocking nagging voice.)
You're not wearing any underwear! You can't eat that!
You were supposed to wash my clothes! Who cares if
Becky and Ralph know about this or that! Jesus, I
would lose my goddamn mind! What have you been
married…like 15 years? 20 years? And it wasn't like
this at the beginning, was it?
(He begins pacing.)
No, I bet it was all sunshine and gumdrops at the
beginning. Courtship's all bullshit posturing…but you
go through it anyway, and it gives you the illusion of
love. You have a big Texas wedding and everybody,
family and friends, shows up and is beaming with joy
and hope. You go on an expensive honeymoon, get the
little two-bedroom apartment, and have lots of
newlywed sex. Great first couple of years, right? Oh,
but then the quirks start to come in, don't they? Little
changes in appearance or demeanor that seem petty
and small at the time, so you overlook them, but at the
same time they're still in the back of your mind,
boiling…festering. Then, 20 years slips by and
now…every little thing sends you into a fevered

frenzy, even in a public place...because you just don't care anymore! You've put up with enough through the years! You've let too much slide and now, by God, you may not have told him you were unhappy with the marriage ten or twelve years ago, and wanted a divorce, but you will let him know how much his not wearing underwear absolutely sickens you, won't you? Jesus, why do we do this to ourselves!

(TOMMY then takes a big drink from the drink he just bought.)

GERALD

(Standing right in front of TOMMY now, visibly upset, clenched fists.)

Are you finished?

TOMMY

Sir, I'm sorry, but I am in the middle of the closest thing I've ever had to a crisis, and you were kind of in the path of the tornado, but you also made clear a very difficult situation.

GERALD

I'm glad I could be of some help.

(Looking outside)

Is that your VW bug outside?

TOMMY

Yes. Why?

GERALD

Margaret. Get in the car.

TOMMY

(Realizing his fate. Now talks to the audience.)

You see? This is why the whole "open and honest society" idea often does not work.

(The scene ends with GERALD punching TOMMY in the face.)

END SCENE 3

Jeremey W. Gingrich

SCENE 4—*Fort Worth, TX The Rehearsal Dinner. This is a scene with a dinner table all set up facing the audience. It is the main table at a wedding reception rehearsal dinner. It is a long table with REGGIE sitting in the middle next to his bride-to-be MADELINE. Sitting next to MADELINE is her Father, FRANK. Sitting next to REGGIE is his father, ROBERT, and to the right of Robert is his wife, TAMMY. FRANK's wife, CONNIE is sitting to his left and another girl, MADDIE's sister VICKI. To the right of TAMMY is TOMMY, on the outskirts, looking in. For this scene, TOMMY gets up out of his chair, with a very visible black eye, after a little while of the usual dinner chitchat, a very short while, TOMMY wipes his mouth and begins talking to the audience.*

TOMMY

(Walking up to the front of the stage.)

You see, this is the problem I have with weddings. You see this place?

(Looks around, motions to the whole room.)

This is a nice place. First class. Ice sculpture next to the bar, chandelier, classy carpets, but it's still somewhat sub-par.

(Pointing back to the table.)

The James family has plugged a lot of money into this affair, and it's just not doing it for me. The problem is, I've watched "The Godfather" like eight million times, and that is the wedding to which I measure all others to this day. At the beginning, when Connie marries Carlo…that's how a wedding should be. Anything less…it's unfulfilling for me. You know, you got everybody there, family friends, family enemies, famous people. The Godfather is taking meetings but still takes the family picture and dances with the bride. Mike's there in his uniform and Fredo's a little drunk. Live band with everybody singing…Oh and that Italian song…

(Italian singing of the song "Lazy Mary.")

Che la luna mensu mare Mama Mia de Marinare. I have yet to go to a wedding where they've sang that

232

song…That's a great song. Oh, yeah, sorry about the sidebar…Intros.

(He goes back to the table stands next to VICKI)
This is Victoria James. She's Madeline's younger sister. Just turned sixteen a few months ago. Word around the campfire is the present she was given for her Sweet Sixteen was Collagen implants in her lips. Sixteen and already with the plastic surgery! Apparently her goal was to look like Mick Jagger. I heard that Collagen in the lips leads to added skills in oral sex…and according to Madeline, we need only ask the offensive line of Vicki's high school football team to test the accuracy of that statement.

(Moves next to CONNIE.)
This is Madeline's mother Constance Marie James. Everyone just calls her Connie. She's a decent lady, and apparently quite a looker back in her day. She gets along really well with Reggie, but then Reg always did well with the mothers over the years. I think some of the mothers of his past girlfriends still send him Christmas cards.

(Moves to FRANK)
Now this is the barracuda. Frank James. Frank is one of those Barbarians at the Gate that had their cake and ate it too back in the eighties, making millions and crushing his competition. Now, what I don't know about corporate America could just about fill the Grand Canyon, but one thing I do know, is that if you cross paths with this man, it's best to cash in your chips and leave the table. I can't fault the man, though. He's using the money to make a better life for his children, and can afford a pretty decent wedding for one daughter, though sub-par by "Godfather" standards, and new lips for the other daughter. The thing is, I think he uses his business practices to also handle his personal affairs. And in my humble opinion, you can't handle people the way you handle corporations.

233

(He skips over MADDIE and REGGIE, moves to the Green family.)

Now these guys here...I'm gonna build a shrine to them one day. This is Robert and Tammy Green, the parents every kid fantasizes about. They smoke, they drink, they swear like a couple of sailors, and they think Bob Dylan is God himself. In college, Reggie and I used to stay with them on the weekends, because the house was only like an hour away from the campus. Far enough for Reg to live in the dorms, but close enough for us to have a homey place to crash on the weekends. She used to make this casserole with mashed potatoes and ground beef...Hamburger Pie she called it, and I swear I could have eaten gallons of that shit. We'd listen to old Dylan albums and play Trivial Pursuit or Uno until 4 in the morning, just drinking and laughing, and dissecting Dylan's lyrics, another one of their favorite pastimes.

(Nostalgic thinking.)

That's what family should be like: people you want to spend time with, that you genuinely enjoy spending time with.

(Looks nostalgically at them, caught in a moment.)

Now, to the bride and groom.

(Moves to Madeline.)

Maddie is a great lady. She's educated, funny, she comes from a well-to-do family yet still remains grounded in reality. And for the most part she seems cool. Coolness is a great thing for a wife to have, because the last thing you want to do is spend the rest of your life with someone who's going to be uptight or rigid about things. One degree of coolness I enjoyed hearing about was when Reggie told me Maddie gave him a blowjob in the back row of a movie theater. Reggie, being the movie fan that he is, found it extremely delightful to mesh two things he enjoys so much together at once. Granted, not every woman has

to do that to be considered a good wife, but I think it goes a long way. And now on to Reggie…
                    REGGIE
          (Interrupting, still sitting in his chair)
Don't you start talking shit about me!
                    TOMMY
What are you doing? You can't interrupt my monologue! Shut up!
                    REGGIE
I can't believe you told them about Maddie in the movie theater! I told you not to tell anybody!
                    TOMMY
Oh, come on! You know that was like one of the proudest moments of your life, you were dying for me to spread the word. I think Tammy…
          (Motions to REGGIE's mom TAMMY)
…was the most impressed, though.
                    REGGIE
You told my mother?
                    TOMMY
Just kidding, just kidding. Relax. And shut up will you, this is not a dialogue. This is my time to shine.
                    REGGIE
Alright, but make it quick. We're having Bananas Foster for dessert.
                    TOMMY
Ooh.
          *(REGGIE sits back down and resumes muted
          conversation with the group at the table. TOMMY
          resumes his monologue.)*
                    TOMMY
Well, that's about it for Reggie. That sums up what we've been for one another these past eight years. The moments I most remember have come out of conflict. Meaningless little arguments based on practically nothing, which have helped us both grow into the responsible, upstanding citizens you see before you. One time, in a Denny's in Colorado Springs, we

underwent a heated discussion as to who would perform better sexually, Jesus Christ or Satan. Reggie figured Satan, stating that he would be extremely naughty and pleasures of the flesh are kind of his department. But I figured Jesus has some hidden talent, because his is usually the name that's called out during sex anyway.

(Fake orgasm.)

Oh Jesus! Oh, Jesus Christ! Anyway, this insane, highly blasphemous argument managed to peak the interest of the cook and three different waitresses, each with their own opinion, and each of them feeling equally disgusted with themselves after voicing that opinion. And…no matter what the argument is, no matter the setting or the participants, there is always laughter. On some occasions, laughter to the point of tears. You can't quantify how much it means to have someone like that as your best friend. A person who challenges you in all sorts of indescribable ways, and also makes you laugh.

(Pause)

You know I've recently completed reading The Adventures of Huckleberry Finn by Mark Twain. Sure, we all know that Michael Caine actually read the book to me, but for all intents and purposes, I'm certainly not going to tell anybody that. One story I remember from the book, one that stuck with me through the drive, was one in which Huck snuck into a circus. I've always liked the circus, and the story Huck tells that really captured my attention was one in which a wild horse was brought to the center ring, a horse so wild, none of the trained riders thought they could tame it. But then a drunkard from the crowd starts proclaiming that he is a better rider than all them put together and that he could tame that horse no problem. The crowd gets angry at the drunken man, but before they erupt into violence and throw him out, the ringmaster says that he'll let the man ride, just so there won't be any trouble. The crowd laughs at the suggestion, with the full confidence that this drunk fool will surely be killed. But then, as the horse starts to rip and tear and thrash about to try to throw this man, the man manages to ride the horse around the ring, astonishing the crowd. Then this supposed drunkard stands up on top of the horse! He stands up! And the crowd is amazed. Then, of course, the man tears off his tattered clothes to reveal a bright colorful circus performers outfit, and the crowd laughs in delight, while the ringmaster blushes with embarrassment. Now, the only reason this story sticks with me at all, besides my love of the circus and fear of horses, is that Huck truly thinks the ringmaster had no idea that was going to happen. He believes that the whole stunt was conjured up by the rider, and that the ringmaster had no advanced knowledge of this exploit. If I were to see that kind of thing at a circus now, I would know for certain that it was a stunt cooked up by the ringmaster, that he is the man pulling the strings to make all of his performers dance, and that nothing comes as a surprise to him. And even though I'd enjoy the show, Huck and kids like him would enjoy it that much more. There is a freedom in youthful ignorance that lets us simply enjoy the things we see in life. This same youthful ignorance protects us from the difficult decisions we have to make as we get older…and even though those decisions may be made with the best interest of all those involved in mind…

(He looks back to the table.)

…We still wish to God we didn't have to make them.

END SCENE 4
END ACT ONE
CURTAIN

Act Two

SCENE 1—*Fort Worth, TX. This is a room in the church in Fort Worth. There is a door on one side of the room that leads out to the altar it has a little latch lock on it. There is a mirror and some chairs, and a little make up table and sink. There is a window that opens out to the outside, it must be big enough for them to climb out and in. On the sink are hair care products and mouthwash and toothbrush. REGGIE and TOMMY are in tuxedos and TOMMY is sweating like you wouldn't believe. He is sitting on the opposite side of the stage, wringing his hands. REGGIE is in front of the mirror, primping. He's putting on cologne and singing.*

REGGIE

(Singing the last verse of "Strangers in the Night.")
"Ever since that night, we've been together. Lovers at first sight, in love forever. It turned out so right for strangers in the night.

> *(Very accentuated and phony Sinatra voice)*

Do Be do be do da da da de da…

> *(Presenting himself to TOMMY)*

What do you think, champ? We talkin' GQ material here, or what?

TOMMY

> *(Uncomfortable laugh)*

Great. We look great.

REGGIE

Damn right.

> *(Back to mirror)*

How we doin' on attendance?

TOMMY

> *(Goes to the door and peers out a little.)*

Well, it's not Yankee Stadium, but it's pretty close. Are all these people going to the reception, too?

REGGIE

(Now brushing his teeth. Pausing and spitting to talk)

238

It's how the big fish live, my friend. They invite all the other big fish to come see their lavish affair. It's not a wedding. To them, it's a competition. They spend WAY too much money, do it up real big, and that raises the bar for the next fish, who of course has to top that. Meanwhile, you and I and the other little fish playing our small yet intricate parts, are merely incidental to their need to show off to one another. But hey, my parents are loving every minute of it, and most of our friends will get to eat better than they have in years. I think they all brought pieces of Tupperware for leftovers. I say at the end of the night we throw it all on the ground and watch 'em go at it like a pack of dogs.

                    TOMMY
Is Mr. James' money gonna be a problem?

                    REGGIE
We've discussed this, haven't we?

                    TOMMY
You know me, I hardly ever really listen to you.

                    REGGIE
Cute. No, Frank and Connie agreed to help us out a little with some starting out money. You know, the ring kind of put a dent in my nest egg. Maddie's got that job up in Denver, and the paper said they're gonna try to option out my column to more publications…so we should do fine. And besides, I am a pretty self-reliant person, but I'm not going to live a sub-par lifestyle out of pride. If we need money, we're going to ask for it. What the hell, I mean they can't take it with them, right?

                    TOMMY
I should try to work that into the wedding toast. But you know how money messes up things. It could turn out like the Mafia. You'll borrow just a little, then pay it back, then a little more, then a little more, then you can't pay him back, then you're under his thumb.

Pretty soon, you're the biggest contract killer on the West Coast. I've seen it a million times.

REGGIE

Money is only a problem if people try to guilt you into paying them back. In order for guilt to work, you have to care. When it comes to they're money...I simply don't care. They got the money to put on a reception with Filet Mignon for 200 guests, just to show off, and there are people starving in the streets. I'm not gonna have a problem asking for money. You think I should gel it back for the wedding?

(Holding hair gel)

TOMMY

I don't know, she may want to run her hand through your hair when you're dancing. You don't want her hand coming out with that shit on it, do you?

REGGIE

Good point. I'll go with a simple comb-back. Hey, all the guys were real impressed with the bachelor party last night. I swear, that club you took us to must have had two hundred fine women dancin' around. And you, pulling and plucking girl after girl from all over the club to come to our table, to see the guy who's getting married. I felt like a freak show. But hey, four of the guys left with chicks from that place. I think they want to build a shrine in your honor.

TOMMY

Tell them I accept all major credit cards as well.

REGGIE

And how did you find that strip club after that anyway? By the end of the night, you knew all the hot spots in Fort Worth. I'd have sworn you'd lived here for the past few years.

TOMMY

I tipped a bellhop at the hotel who looked like he knew of certain establishments. What about you, did you like the strip club here compared to the ones back home?

REGGIE

Well, yeah, I mean that goes without question. The place last night had twice as many girls and better drinks. But there's a certain homey feeling to the ones we had back in Colorado.

TOMMY

It's a feeling that comes when all the girls call out your name when you walk into the place.

REGGIE

(Nostalgically)

Yeah, I swear I think we put two or three of those girls through college.

TOMMY

And some of them tried to milk us for a Masters Degree.

REGGIE

Remember the night the DJ did movie trivia for lap dances? He had to disqualify us. The ladies were getting fed up.

TOMMY

I guess he didn't count on our endless knowledge of things that really don't matter in life. Let me ask you something, you ever gonna try to take Madeline to a strip club?

REGGIE

What you mean like for Amateur night or something?

TOMMY

No, just to go with you. Sit and watch, maybe get a lap dance…You think you'd do that.

REGGIE

I don't think so.

TOMMY

Why not? You had fun when you went there, didn't you?

REGGIE

Well, yeah.

TOMMY

So, why should there be a place that you enjoy that you
can't share with your wife? Doesn't that seem strange,
I mean if married people are supposed to share things.

REGGIE

But that's different. I mean, you saw the guys that
brought their girlfriends into the place back home, hell
even last night. What did we think of those women?
We used to think they were trash. We used to say, why
would she let him take her here? Doesn't she have any
self-respect? I don't want people thinking that about
Maddie.

TOMMY

So will you still go to the clubs yourself?

REGGIE

Yeah, definitely.

TOMMY

And what is she doing while you're out at the club?
Sitting at home? Then one night she asks why you
have to go to this club, why can't you stay home with
her? Pretty soon, you're not going to the place you
enjoyed because of her. Won't that foster some
resentment? I mean, I'm just asking, that's all.

REGGIE

Yes...

(He looks out the door at the guests)

...and at such an opportune time. What are you trying
to say? You've known me for too long to be so obtuse,
just say it.

TOMMY

(Real jittery and very nervous)

Hey, Reg, I'm not trying to say anything. You know
me, I often have no point...but well, I heard about this
couple once. Family friends-that's how I know them.
They got married at around 27, 26..I forget
which...well, the guy was 26...the girl was only
22...and they got married and the first years were just

fine. But because they were still young with a lot of the world left to explore, they started to wonder about the things they were missing out on. Then, as they became more successful and got to know more people, they started to think, maybe I'd have been happier with her, or her, or him...or whatever. Next thing you know they were divorced, and their kids...their kids get split up on Thanksgiving and Christmas, and they harbor deep hatred and resentment towards their parents. I think that's how the Menendez kids got so fucked up. But this couple is now split up and miserable. But the misery could have been avoided if they'd have waited a little longer, experienced a little more, before they got married...at least that's what my mother told me...about these long time family friends. That's a story my mom recently told me and it made me think...that's all. I was just thinking out loud.

REGGIE
(Laughing slightly, then goes to the sink. Splashes some water on his face. Looks up at TOMMY then starts laughing again. Then stops.)
You piece of shit.

TOMMY
What?

REGGIE
You piece of chicken shit. This is what you've become? This is my Best Man? You are my most trusted friend, my Best...You're the Best Man at my wedding!! For fuck's sake! And this is how you tell me you have a problem with me getting married? You make up a fictional fucking married couple? What the fuck is that?

TOMMY
Well, actually it was this guy in New Mexico...

REGGIE
And the timing...Oh, my friend...the timing is fucking brilliant!

243

(Looks at his watch)

The invitation tells you what time I'm getting married, I'm somewhat sure of that. And I'm pretty sure I told you…maybe eight million fucking times, Noon on Saturday. But no, you still decide to wait until that exact time to tell me that you think this is a big fucking mistake? What's the matter? Too afraid to bring up your little hypothetical situation in front of the whole fucking congregation? If you were going for last minute, I think that's technically the best time.

TOMMY

You think this was easy for me? You think this is like ordering a fucking sandwich? I'm basically telling you I think the most important decision you will ever make in your life, is perhaps the dumbest thing you could do with your life. I've been wrestling with this thing too fucking long for you to belittle it like that, motherfucker. And as for timing, what the hell is the best time, Ms. Manners? When? At the rehearsal dinner? Hey, Reggie, I think you're throwing your life away, can you pass the fucking salt? Doesn't have a nice ring, does it?

REGGIE

Easy for you? Who the hell cares if this was easy for you? You get a few butterflies in your stomach…

TOMMY

Try projectile vomiting, okay? Those were not butterflies.

REGGIE

A little projectile vomiting, and I'm supposed to feel sorry for you? This is my wedding day, Tommy! My wedding day! This is not about you! You think I'm not a little scared about this decision? That's what the Best Man is for; he's supposed to calm me down so I can keep a clear head in front of two hundred plus people who came here today to see a wedding! Instead, you're showing me the fucking door!

(Points at the door.)
(Just then the door opens and REGGIE's dad,
ROBERT, peaks in. He is wearing a tux as well.)
REGGIE
(Surprised and wanting to sound calm and relaxed)
Dad! Hey, what's happening?
ROBERT
Son, it's about that time. You need to take your spot up
at the altar. *(Looks to TOMMY)* Is everything, alright?
TOMMY
Yes, Robert, everything's fine. We're just going to
need a minute…I…lost a contact lens…shouldn't be
but a moment.
(Now he is looking down for his contact. This line
works well for people without glasses, but I think it's a
little funnier if the actor has glasses.)
ROBERT
(Starts to close the door then opens it again.)
But you don't wear…
REGGIE
(Closing the door on his father.)
We just need two seconds, dad. Thanks.
(The door is closed.)
I love my dad, Tommy. Do you know how
disappointed he's going to be if I don't go out there?
He came to me last night with tears in his eyes, to tell
me how proud he was…
TOMMY
I can appreciate that it would be a hard thing to do, but
I also realize that as soon as I brought up my little
hypothetical situation, you could have told me I was
way off base and walked out there already. The fact
that you insist on cursing my doubts, and flailing about
like a madman, says to me that you're trying to
convince yourself to go through with it.
REGGIE
Like I give a fuck what it says to you…

TOMMY

And, you know I think the world and all of Robert,
both your parents, Jesus, I wouldn't have made it
through college if it wasn't for you guys, and you
know this! But every one of those people out there, to
include your parents who we both love, doesn't matter
worth shit! Not worth shit! Because it's not their life.
They don't have to wake up next to this person every
morning of every day for the rest of their lives. That's
you, buddy! For the rest of your life! The worst thing
you could do is take anybody out there into
consideration when making this decision, if you have
doubts. And, to me, it looks like you have doubts! And
yes, I know this isn't the best time to say so! And yes, I
know it makes me the worst Best Man in the history of
the title! But I don't fucking care! If that's what it
means, I'll take being a good friend to being a good
Best Man any day.

REGGIE

This is being a good friend? Whatever happened to
support? Whatever happened to loyalty? That's what I
need here, Tommy! Not marital advice from someone
who's never even had a woman for a period longer
than 6 months!

TOMMY

If you don't see this as loyalty and support than you
are fucking blind, man! I'm trying to prevent you from
making a disastrous mistake here, or at least to
consider the possibility that it's a mistake! As far as
weddings go, I often see people get so wrapped up in
the pageantry of the ceremony, of the importance of
the one-day, they forget about the permanence of the
decision they make there.

REGGIE

And what would you have me do, sprint out the church
doors? Or, no, let me guess, something more dramatic,

right? Dustin Hoffman in "The Graduate?" Fight
people back with the church cross?
                    TOMMY
Oh, for Christ's sake don't get crazy.
                    (Pause)
We couldn't go out that door at all. We'd have to crawl
out the window.
                    REGGIE
I can see it now, National Lampoon's Wedding Day.
                    TOMMY
          (Close to him, hand on his shoulder.)
Look, I'm just worried about you, alright?
          (REGGIE's rage is dying a bit.)
Jesus, you're the best friend I got.
*(He hugs him, REGGIE just stands there. Then, as he
is about to succumb and hug him back, he pushes him
        away instead and fixes his tux.)*
                    REGGIE
Okay, best friend. Slap a smile on for the ceremony,
will you? No long faces in the wedding photos.
          *(He's goes to the door and puts his hand on the
                    doorknob.)*
And are you gonna straighten up and fly right by the
reception, or should I have my father give the toast.
                    TOMMY
              (Head down. Defeated.)
Better…Better to get Robert to do it. I'm…I'm sorry.
     *(REGGIE looks at him a bit longer, then opens the
          door, pauses…shuts the door.)*
                    REGGIE
Alright, let's get out of here. You gotta drive.
                    TOMMY
No problem, I've got my keys.
*(They head for the window, TOMMY opens it and gets
          one leg out.)*
                    REGGIE
Wait, wait, wait! This is ridiculous!

                    TOMMY
What?

                    REGGIE
(Pause, as he straightens up and breathes a little. He
then runs to the door and locks the bolt.)
This will buy us more time. Go, go!
(TOMMY crawls out the window and REGGIE follows
after.)

END SCENE 1

SCENE 2—*Decatur, TX. Another McDonald's on the road. This*
has the same set-up as the last one, basically. We can pivot the set a
little if we'd like, but all the elements of the place are the same. There
is a counter from which to order, a separate counter from which to
procure condiments and napkins, and there are three tables set aside
for people to sit. One couple, TONIA and PETE are already seated
and eating. TOMMY and REGGIE are in line behind one guy
ordering his food. They are still in tuxes, but without the coats. Just
the vests and bow ties. Behind the counter is a twerpy kid, ALEX,
about 17, with a bit of an attitude, not so much that you would notice
it at first, but it comes out when provoked. There is also a manager,
THOMPSON, who wears a shirt and tie and seems like an alright
guy. He is working in the background at the beginning of the scene. In
the beginning, ALEX takes the order from the man in line in front of
the guys, BOB, and then goes to prepare it.
                    REGGIE
                (Solemn, banal)
Thanks for stopping for some food. I haven't eaten all
day.
                    TOMMY
It's no problem, really.
                    REGGIE
Well, I know you like to make good time when you're
on long drives…you're not real prone to frequent
stops.

TOMMY
I'm getting into the habit.
*(ALEX has come back to the counter and handed a
tray to BOB who has a newspaper under his arm and
thanks ALEX then sits at one of the tables.)*
ALEX
(To REGGIE and TOMMY)
What'll it be, fellas?
REGGIE
Yeah, could I get two double-hamburgers with no
pickle?
(Now, to TOMMY)
You getting a meal?
TOMMY
Yeah.
REGGIE
Super-size it, will ya? We'll just split the fries and
drink.
(Back to ALEX)
Yeah, just two double-hamburgers, no pickle and
whatever he's having.
*(REGGIE slides a bit over to the left, then TOMMY
scoots in closer to the counter.)*
TOMMY
And could I get a Number 4, super sized with Sprite,
and a cheeseburger. Thanks.
*(ALEX goes to prep the food. TOMMY looks at
REGGIE who is kind of looking at the floor.)*
REGGIE
(Looking at the floor.)
You know what I was thinking about…as we were
sneaking away from the church…I remembered that
one time we were cheating on a test on American
History.
TOMMY
Which one? Before Civil War or after?

REGGIE

After. You remember, when we usually cheated we'd put our books in the bathroom nearest to the test room, and we'd just keep making trips back and forth, reading the questions and then looking up the answers.

TOMMY

Yeah, but on one of the tests we brought the wrong book, so you had to run back to the room and get the right one...

REGGIE

And the professor saw me running around campus and questioned me after the test. Man, I thought he was gonna kick me out of the class. But then you came up and made up this story about your inhaler.

(Laughing.)

TOMMY

Yeah, I borrowed Ted Davis' inhaler and said it was mine, and that I'd forgotten it and you had to run back to the room and grab it for me. 'Cause I was having an attack during the test.

(They are in full laughter now.)

And you picked up the cue and just rolled with it. That was priceless.

(ALEX comes with the tray of food. TOMMY is about to take it.)

REGGIE

Just a second.

(He takes one of his burgers out of the wrapper. Then the other. Very calm)

Yep. This happens sometimes.

(To ALEX, still calm)

Um, excuse me, sir. I asked for double hamburgers, please. These have cheese.

(He places the burgers back down on the tray.)

ALEX

(With a sigh.)

Just a minute.

(He takes the burgers and deliberately throws them away. Goes to prep two new ones)
REGGIE

It was good to get a laugh. Take my mind off of...
(ALEX comes back with two more burgers.)
ALEX

Here ya go, no cheese.
(Attitude)
REGGIE

We got the pickles off there too, right?
ALEX
(Sigh)
You wanted no pickles on these, too?
REGGIE
(Still calm)
Don't worry about it. I'll just pick 'em off.
(He grabs the tray and starts to walk off but then ALEX mumbles something a little incoherent but everyone knows he said something. REGGIE stops and puts the tray back down.)
What was that? I didn't quite catch it?
ALEX

Nothing...Well, I was just curious why you'd take off the pickles, but not the cheese.
REGGIE

What?

TOMMY

Come on. Let's just eat.
(TOMMY grabs the tray.)
REGGIE

No.
(To TOMMY)
Put that down.
(Back to ALEX)
What's the problem?
ALEX

Look, I don't want any trouble...

251

REGGIE

No, no, you seem to know more about my eating habits than I do…Let's hear it?

ALEX

(Attitude showing up.)

Well, it's just that, I had to throw those last two burgers away, you know? And if you'd just scrape off the cheese, like you're so willing to do with the pickles…

REGGIE

Oh, man, did you pick a shitty day!

TOMMY

Just let it lie, will you?

REGGIE

No.

(He grabs the cheeseburger from the tray.)

Give me this.

(He opens the wrapper, takes out the burger then takes off the bun, doing irreparable damage to the burger.)

You see this, sporty? This is why you can't scrape off the cheese. You got some kind of nuclear meltdown happenin' as soon as you put cheese on these things, alright! As soon as you make a cheeseburger, it finds a way to stay a cheeseburger! The cheese clings to the bread, and even when you try to scrape off the cheese with a paper-thin razor blade you end up with a yellow film on the meat!

(He slams the burger down onto the counter.)

TOMMY

Are you listening to yourself? Are we having this conversation?

(THOMPSON, the manager, hears the exchange and joins in on ALEX's side of the counter.)

THOMPSON

Is anything the matter, sir.

REGGIE

No, no problem at all.

252

(Obviously sarcastic)
We got the employee of the month, here, how can
there be a problem?

ALEX

Look, Thompson, I don't know what the problem is?
These guys apparently took time off from valet parking
to hassle me.

REGGIE

Oh, that's cute.

TOMMY

Look, Mr. Thompson, it's really nothing important...

THOMPSON

It's not Mr. Thompson, sir. Its just Thompson.

TOMMY

Really? People call you Tom for short?

THOMPSON

No. Just Thompson. Like the water seal. What can I do
for you?

TOMMY

*(REGGIE has succumbed to the situation and grabbed
the tray and gone to the condiments table.)*
My friend just has passionate views on the
cheeseburger, that's all.
*(Looking down at the crumbled mess that REGGIE has
made his cheeseburger into that is still on the counter.)*
Speaking of which, could I possibly get another one?
My first one was a casualty of the conversation.

THOMPSON

Sure, no problem.

(To ALEX)
Alex, could you please get this gentleman another
cheeseburger?
*(ALEX is eyeballing REGGIE at the condiment
counter, who is shooting him spiteful glances as well,
he then goes to get TOMMY his cheeseburger.)*

Not that we don't appreciate it, sir, but you seem a
little overdressed for our humble establishment. But
not as a valet, I assure you.

TOMMY
(Looking down at his outfit.)

Oh, long story. We're just driving through and we like
to look good for the road.

THOMPSON

I don't know, you guys are too old to be heading to the
Prom. And it's early in the day for a black tie affair. If
I had to guess…

TOMMY

And you really don't.

THOMPSON

I'd say you were on your way to a wedding.
(ALEX comes with TOMMY's burger.)
Am I right?
*(TOMMY takes the burger and puts his finger up to his
mouth, shushing THOMPSON, as he walks to the table
that REGGIE has sat at.)*
No, that's what it is, isn't it? That's great! Who's
getting married?
(REGGIE just eats his food with his head down.)
TOMMY

It's nobody, really. I mean…it's nothing.

THOMPSON

Nothing?
*(He comes from behind the counter into the eating
area, grabs the chair from the table next to theirs and
sits in it.)*
What are you talking about? Weddings are great!
Whole family's there. Church packed with friends and
relatives from all over. Big reception with food and
drinks…Dancing and music. All based around two
people's love for one another. I really envy you two.

254

TOMMY
(Looking at REGGIE shaking his head. To
THOMPSON.)
That's the image of marriage Hallmark tries to sell
you. But what about the opposite, huh? What if the
whole time you're sitting through the ceremony, you
are consumed with the fact that the two people whose
love has brought everybody together, are throwing
their lives away! That the next twenty years of their
lives, if it lasts that long…a rarity in our time…will be
spent in childish bickering, miserable compromising,
and dreadfully monogamous monogamy!
THOMPSON
The average person doesn't think that when he's
marrying the woman he loves. My wedding day, 16
years ago, was a day filled with…
TOMMY
The average person isn't thinking when he marries the
woman he loves! Especially before the age of 35! Why
on earth would a rational man settle for just one
woman for the rest of his natural life!
THOMPSON
But it's not settling if it's the woman you love!
(TOMMY gets up and paces a bit.)
REGGIE
Tommy, just let it go…
TOMMY
No, wait just a second.
(To THOMPSON)
We being frank here?
THOMPSON
It's the only way growth is truly experienced.
TOMMY
After you got married, did you still masturbate?
(REGGIE spits out the drink he just drank.)
THOMPSON
Okay…

(Gets up)
…I think that's maybe too frank.
TOMMY
No, no. There's no such thing. Frankness is not measured in degrees. Come on…Growth!
THOMPSON
(Gathering his reserve)
Okay. Fine. Yes…I did still…you know…after I was married.
TOMMY
Who were you thinking about while you were…
(Makes the masturbation motion)
…working? Your wife? Be honest.
THOMPSON
Sometimes…
REGGIE
And the other times?
THOMPSON
Well…the Bangles.
TOMMY
(Smiles)
Alright, the Bangles. Very cool. Which one? The lead singer?
THOMPSON
Actually it was kind of all four at once…
REGGIE
Is that all?
THOMPSON
(Awkward)
And I had this thing for Linda Carter.
TOMMY
Wonder Woman?
THOMPSON
Yep.
(Lost in the fantasy, wakes up from it.)
Wait a minute…Why the hell does that matter?

TOMMY

Well, alright, say you ran into Linda Carter after you were married? Say she was shooting a movie here in…Where are we?

REGGIE

Decatur.

TOMMY

Here in Decatur, Texas and you bumped into her. And she found you witty and charming and you found her grounded and gorgeous…You already fantasize about her, wouldn't you rather be with her than with your wife?

THOMPSON

Well, yeah, but…

TOMMY

But that would never happen right? You accepted the fact that even though you were more attracted to this woman than your own wife, you would probably never meet her…So you settled for the woman you married, and just kept fantasizing about the woman you'd rather be with, if you were only lucky enough to meet her. Marriage is the acceptance of the idea that, "Hey, I'm just not able to do any better."

THOMPSON

Jesus Christ.

(Defeated)
(REGGIE gets up and leads THOMPSON back behind the counter.)

REGGIE

Relax, don't take it personally. He's just doing what he thinks is right to help me come to terms with my decision. I just left my bride at the altar in front of 250 people just an hour ago.

THOMPSON, TONIA, PETE, and BOB
(Altogether now)

You did what?

REGGIE

That's why we're dressed like this. He's the Best Man.
We ran out of the church, hustled back to the hotel,
threw my suitcases in the car and booked on out of
there. I left a lot of things behind, but I'm writing those
off as losses, because I wasn't going to stay behind and
face those people today.

TONIA

Let me get this straight, you leave this woman at the
altar, effectively ruining her life, then book it out of
there as fast as your legs will carry you…and then find
yourself in the mood for a cheeseburger?

REGGIE

No cheese.

TONIA

So what, now you're hiding out in Decatur?

REGGIE

No, we're on our way back to Denver, we just stopped
for…for the food. But now that's the part I'm worried
about.

PETE

What part is that?

REGGIE

Well, my friend here has gone through this whole
exercise here…

(Looking at THOMPSON, still depressed at his
newfound revelation.)

…which has made this man an utter shambles, because
he thinks I have regrets about the decision I made
today. What he forgets is that I rarely trouble myself
with thoughts of regret, as they are seldom helpful.
But, now that I have had time to clear my head, the
emotion that takes over now is fear. Paralyzing,
agonizing fear!

(Working up to a panic)

TOMMY

Why? Of what?

REGGIE

Tommy, this woman knows where I live! Maddie
knows where we live! I hideously embarrassed her in
front of her family and friends...hell in front of half of
the Texas elite! She's going to toss Molotov cocktails
though our windows every day for the next three
weeks! We're going to have to get flame-retardant
furniture and like eighteen fire extinguishers!

TOMMY

You're overreacting.

REGGIE

Oh, am I? Not only am I the guy directly responsible
for humiliating this girl on what was supposed to be
the greatest day of her life...but I got her father to pay
for all of it! The church, the reception, all the
limousines...we flew in people from all over the
country...from as far away as Maine, Tommy! Maine!
All of it totaling one hundred and seventeen thousand-
six hundred and twenty four dollars!

EVERYBODY

JESUS CHRIST!

TOMMY

A hundred and twenty thousand doll...

REGGIE

No, my friend. One hundred and seventeen thousand-
six hundred and twenty four dollars. Daddy Dearest
was very insistent that I remember the exact figure.
And as much as he says it's about his daughter,
Frank's going to see this as a personal insult to him!
His money, in front of his society friends...He's going
to kill me!

BOB

Yeah, I could see that.

REGGIE

Thanks for those two cents...But this is a man with
power, Thomas! Men with money and power are
permitted like one guilt-free murder in their lives!

Look at Gary Condit! O.J Simpson! And this is Texas, you know! Frank James is a Texan! These people actually encourage death as a form of conflict resolution! He could kill me, get caught, and then get elected Governor!

TOMMY

Alright, that's enough! Sit down here, you're going to start hyperventilating.

(REGGIE sits, eating fries.)

Okay, this is what is going to happen! We, you and I, are going to drive back to Denver. We're going to continue our lives as normal. Maddie will have to take some recovery time, she'll probably stay down in Texas with her folks for a while. We have caller ID, thank God, so we just won't answer any calls from the Texas area code. You'll have to clear things with your folks, of course, but they're rational people, that won't be a problem. Eventually, she'll come back up to Denver, I mean she did get a job in the city, right? But by that time she'll have had time to calm down and realize that everything that happened…happened for the best. She'll come and talk to you about it, and yes, she'll still be angry, but I don't think death will be involved.

REGGIE

And what about Frank and the…

TOMMY

Yeah, I know, the one hundred and seventeen thousand six-hundred and twenty four dollars.

(Thinking)

Makes one hell of a tax write-off. Trust me, alright, the rich always find a way of making up their losses. He'll be super fuckin' pissed, that's for sure, but he'll spend a day at a spa and get over it. That's what the rich do.

REGGIE

And as for us…

TOMMY

We chalk all this up to experience and go about our
lives like nothing happened. We continue our patterns
of late nights at Denny's and pizza for breakfast. And
if your paper really does option out your column, who
knows, you might hit it big nationally. Make a few
guest spots on various talk shows and voila, all the
women you'll meet will make ol' "what's her face" a
distant memory.

REGGIE

You think I could get on "Regis and Kelly?"

TOMMY

Whoa, hey let's not shoot for the stars, okay? But
you'll do fine.

TONIA

(Who's been eavesdropping obviously.)
Can I just say something here?

REGGIE

Sure.

TONIA

I just wanted to say, before you left, that I think the
two of you might be the most despicable people I've
ever met. The fact that this one ever got anyone to
agree to marry him is unfathomable, but what strains
belief all the more is that you left that woman at the
altar, forever skewing her concepts of trust and love.

(To TOMMY)
And you, in a shameful attempt to validate your
breaking up this one wedding, to try to comfort
yourself after the fact, decided to tear down the whole
institution of marriage itself, irreparably damaging this
poor man's...

*(Motioning to THOMPSON, slouching on the counter,
still thinking about his marriage.)*
...image of his own marriage. Look at him. He's not
going to look at his wife the same way again.

261

TOMMY
Or Wonder Woman, for that matter.
TONIA
So, after witnessing all that…Yes, you might be the
most emotionally bankrupt people I've ever met.
TOMMY
But at least we're well dressed, right?
REGGIE
Look, miss, I won't deny I've done a pretty shitty thing
today, alright? But if you're asking us to feel some sort
of remorse or regret, you're talkin' to the wrong guys.
We don't trouble ourselves with those things because
they never help. All you end up doing is moping
around, saying to yourself, "Why didn't I do this?" or
"I should have done that?"
(To THOMPSON)
It's a waste of time. We embrace and defend our
decisions, especially the bad ones, and sometimes we
tear down some people along the way, but somehow
we manage to sleep pretty well. Despicable traits,
maybe…

TOMMY
…But it certainly makes for one hell of a ride. Let's
get out of here, bud. We got a long drive ahead of us.
(He grabs the soda. REGGIE walks out the door.)
Thompson, you take it easy, buddy. Give our best to
the Mrs.
(TOMMY leaves.)
TONIA
(She gets up and goes over to THOMPSON.)
You aren't going to seriously let those guys effect the
way you go about your marriage, are you?
THOMPSON
(Still thinking)
Of course not. But, I'll tell you one thing, tonight my
wife and I are going to have the best sex we've had in
years.

TONIA

Good for you. That's what you need to do, just keep
the romance alive…

THOMPSON

Yeah…

(Pause)

…but first I'm getting on the Internet and downloading
a shit load of pictures of Linda Carter.

END SCENE 2

SCENE 3—*Goodnight, TX. It is Poetry night at the local truck
stop/bar. Ray's Truck Stop is a bar with a collective area at one point.
There is a stage area with a microphone set up, with tables around it
where people are sitting, drinking and smoking, but their attention is
still on the TV above the bar. There is a large congregation around
the bar staring at the TV, cheering and yelling. RAY is the bartender
and owner of the establishment, other key players amidst the yokels
are BILLY RAY, CLETUS and ROCKY. These are gruff, Texan truck
drivers, with overalls and plaid and T-shirts with beer stuff on them.
The crowd is watching the tail end of a NASCAR race. Country music
is playing in the background.*

RAY

(Turning off the television.)

Well, fellas, that's another end to another fine race
down at Darlington Raceway.

BILLY RAY

(To everybody.)

I'm telling ya, Jeff Gordon, ain't never gonna finish
better than 4th if he don't hold off on that last pit stop.

ROCKY

But how about that Dale Earnhardt Jr.? By God, that
boy's just got them superior racing genes.

(Everybody laughs.)

RAY

(Looking at the clock)

263

Boys, it's eight o'clock. You know what that means.
Come on now, help set up the chairs and such.
*(The guys all move the tables and chairs to all face the
stage. RAY turns off the country music and turns on
some lights that light up the microphone on the stage.
After all the chairs are set up, all the truck drivers take
a seat with their drinks. RAY soon comes up to the
stage.)*
RAY
Fellas, I know you all have driven in from all points on
the map, for one reason or another. But for the most
part you all have come to know this establishment as
your home on the road...And for that I thank you. And
now, before I keep gushing on about you fine people...
(People laugh)
It's time for our weekly night of literary exploration.
First on the list here, is Billy Ray Mitchell. Let's all
welcome him with a warm round of applause.
*(The crowd cheers a little as BILLY RAY steps up to
the microphone.)*
BILLY RAY
(Shy, very Southern accent.)
Hello, everybody. My name is Billy Ray Mitchell, and
tonight I would like to share with you a Haiku poem I
wrote while truckin' through an empty patch of
Tupelo, Mississippi.

*(Clears throat. He says his poem slowly, looking down
at his paper for a moment, then up longingly)*
"The leaves that fall down...Caress the earth and lie
still...As time slowly slips"
*(He bows his head as he says the last words. The
crowd erupts in cheers and mindful and thoughtful
talk. RAY comes back on stage.)*
RAY
That was truly enlightening, Billy Ray. I especially
like the alliteration at the end.

(BILLY RAY sits down.)
And now Rocky Hobgood would like to share a
passage…
*(ROCKY gets up to try to walk towards the stage, but
as he is getting there, TOMMY and REGGIE storm in
through the door, panicked and breathing heavy. They
are still wearing their vests and bow ties around their
necks, though untied.)*

REGGIE
I can't believe it! We're eight hours away, for Christ's
sake!

TOMMY
They tried to run us off the road, Reggie! They tried to
run us off the fucking road! How in the world did they
find us?

REGGIE
(Angry.)
How do you fucking think, genius? You're driving a
Goddamn yellow Volkswagen Bug in Texas! You
wonder how they knew it was us? I think they usually
hang people who drive VW bugs into Texas!

TOMMY
But it's alright, I think! We parked in between those
two big rigs, and ran into this truck…
*(They finally look around at the people, seated in their
forum, all looking at them in the dead silence of the
truck stop.)*
…stop.
*(They stop leaning on the door and walk into the room.
They look around very silently. RAY finally comes up
to them.)*

RAY
Gentlemen, you look as though you come to our
particular establishment with an interesting story to
tell. Rocky, I'm gonna bump you a set, if you don't
mind.

(RAY grabs TOMMY by the arm and leads him to the microphone. ROCKY goes and sits down, not shunned, but eager to hear what the traveler has to say.)
Alright, here ya go. And please, try to watch the language.
(At this remark, CLETUS stands up.)
CLETUS
(Also with a heavy accent, and wearing a trashy shirt. Think "Van Halen")
Profanity is the language of emotion! You can't take that out of artistic expression!
RAY
(Still onstage with TOMMY. REGGIE is looking on, bewildered at what's happening.)
Cletus, sit down!
(To TOMMY)
You'll have to excuse him, sir. Cletus' work is laced with vulgarity. He claims it's the voice of discontent, but really I just think his Momma didn't bring him up right. Now go ahead, start with your name.
(TOMMY looks to REGGIE because he doesn't know what he should do. REGGIE doesn't know either, he throws up his hands in a hopeless and helpless "I don't know" manner.)
TOMMY
(Into the microphone.)
My name is…Tommy. Tommy Maloney. I'm from Denver, Colorado.
(He now covers the microphone. To RAY, who is still standing by him.)
What should I say?
RAY
Tell us your story, son. Answer some of the questions that these crinkled foreheads are asking you.
(Motions out to the audience.)

I look at you and I'm struck with two questions right
off the bat. What's with the monkey suit, and who
gave you the shiner?

(TOMMY feels his eye, almost as if he forgot he had
the black eye.)

TOMMY

Oh, this. Well...

(Again looking to REGGIE, again with the hands up "I
don't know")

...I got this from a devoted husband in a gas station
outside of Dallas.

(The gallery mumbles, talking about the different
possibilities.)

No, it was nothing sexual...I wasn't like sleeping with
his wife or anything. I...it was the end of a long drive
for me. I had to drive from Denver all the way down to
Fort Worth for my friend there. That's Reggie. He was
supposed to be getting married today.

CLETUS

What do you mean, "supposed to be?"

TOMMY

I'm getting to that. I'm trying to have structure here.
So I have this miserable drive through this empty
chasm of a state, and you know how it is, when you're
driving for all that time your mind starts to mess with
you.

ROCKY

No, we don't know anything about that, do we fellas?

(They all laugh)

TOMMY

Yeah, so you know where I'm coming from. So as I
drive, everywhere I stop, for gas or food or what not, I
meet people, just average everyday people, and they
tell me about marriage, because what do I know, you
know? And I'm tugged back and forth between being
supportive and positive or being pragmatic and
realistic. These opinions come from people of all ages,

267

from all types of backgrounds, but the biggest impact…my one true epiphany…came upon meeting an older married couple in a convenient store/gas station. They bickered and fought, she nagged and he looked miserable, and though I realized that not all marriages end up that way, even the chance of my best friend going through one day like that…let alone several years…was crushing. I felt the need to tell this couple that they were the worst pairing since Pam and Tommy Lee, and then the husband felt the need to put his fist through my face. Luckily, my eye was there to stop that from happening. But it was through this cathartic occurrence that I did realize the true purpose behind the trip…And so, today, in a fit of insecure panic…I stopped the wedding.

REGGIE
(Chiming in.)

That's not entirely true.

(He goes up to the stage as well.)

True, he did tell me at the last second that I was making a terrible mistake, but it was me…It was I who made the actual decision. And so now, the truly supportive friend comes out.

(To TOMMY)

You don't get all the credit slash blame on this one, Tommy Boy. But since the whole thing started you've been great. This drive up to Denver, though not even halfway done, could have been an emotional disaster, and at some points it came very close, but you were there, helping me, supporting me and even crushing people along the way, just to make me feel better. You were the voice of reason and stability, which is scary in itself, when I needed it the most…I guess you've always been that. So, as a dénouement to this babbling, I ask you good people of…what is this? Ray's? I ask you to raise your glasses high and pray to whomever

268

you pray to that you're lucky enough to have a man
like this as a friend.
>*(He puts his arm around TOMMY.)*
>*(The truckers all raise their beers in a warm toast.)*
>*(Just then, FRANK JAMES and MADDIE storm
>through the doors. MADDIE is still wearing her
>wedding dress, FRANK still in his tuxedo. They are
>noticeably mad.)*
MADDIE
You fucking bastard!
>*(REGGIE pushes TOMMY away and points at him.)*
REGGIE
It's all his fault!
FRANK
>*(Coming closer. Angry.)*
You've got some nerve treating my girl like this,
asshole. And now you stand there trying to blame…
REGGIE
>*(On the microphone)*
I don't know, Ray? This guy looks like he may be
prone to violence. Is that the kind of place you're
running here?
>*(RAY steps in between FRANK and REGGIE.)*
RAY
He's right, sir.
>*(ROCKY and BILLY RAY stand up around FRANK as
>well.)*
We don't handle our problems like that around here.
BILLY RAY
Why don't you have a seat, sir? I'm sure we can talk
through this.
*(FRANK's rage is quieted by his fear of burly truckers.
He has a seat.)*
MADDIE
Well, I'm not taking a fucking seat! What the hell is
the matter with you?
>*(Close to tears but really upset.)*

Look at me, Reggie! Look at me!
                    TOMMY
Yeah, I meant to say how nice you looked, Maddie.
Great dress.

                    MADDIE
I'm glad you noticed it, Tommy, as you sprinted out
the fucking door!
           (Back to REGGIE)
Do you know how long I've dreamt about my wedding
day? This is the day every girl looks forward to from
the age of 5. We envision the dress, the ceremony, the
flowers…This was supposed to be my dream day,
Reggie! And instead of dancing with my father at my
wedding reception, I am in a fucking truck stop with
the Texas chapter of MENSA, screaming at the man I
was going to marry!

                    RAY
Ma'am, I know you're upset, and it is a truly beautiful
dress, by the way, but if you could try to please watch
your language…

                    FRANK
I don't believe what I'm hearing. Where the hell are
we?

                    MADDIE
Watch my language?
           (In disbelief, asking the truckers.)
Can he see me? Do you see me? Do you see what I'm
wearing? I was supposed to get married today, smart
guy, and I've had to chase the groom half way across
this whole fucking state! This is the language of
emotion!

                    CLETUS
                    (To RAY)
I told you!

                    RAY
Sit down!

TOMMY
(Coming to the forefront. To MADDIE)
Now wait minute! How did you find us anyway? I
mean, not like we're hiding, but this state is pretty
fuc…
(Looks at Ray)
…pretty damn big! We're toolin' along, next thing I
know your stretch limo pulls up, and you're flipping
me the bird out the back seat window.

MADDIE
It's not like your vehicle is inconspicuous, Tommy!
It's a yellow clown car in Texas!

TOMMY
(To the crowd.)
Everybody's knocking my car this week. And speaking
of my car,
(To FRANK)
I don't much appreciate you trying to run me off the
road…

FRANK
Enough! Listen to me! You've got some explaining to
do, mister! At present, I won't tackle the issue of
expense, but I will definitely come to that, but this is
my little girl here.
(To the gallery)
That counts for something, doesn't it? I have a
legitimate gripe here. We've…she's been embarrassed
in front of all her friends, and her mother hasn't
stopped crying since we left, which…
(Motioning to their clothes)
…as you can tell, was right after we pieced together
your little disappearing act. The emotional damage and
mental strain of this one event could have done
irreparable harm to the one person I've spent my whole
life trying to protect. Come on, guys! Just let me take
him out back and shoot him, will ya? Just once!
(To RAY)

271

You gotta have something behind the bar, right? Just a small gun? I'll only shoot him in the kneecap, he'll live.

(REGGIE cowers behind everyone near him.)

TOMMY

You heard the man, fellas. Threatening physical violence in a public place! You're our witnesses! This man is a lunatic. You tried to run me off the fucking road!

RAY

Tommy!

TOMMY

Sorry, Ray. Last one, I promise. The way I drive…You could've killed us!

FRANK

I didn't try to run you off the road!

TOMMY

What?

FRANK

…My driver did. He's a good man, he does what I tell him. And he's waiting in the car right now.

TOMMY

Well, then I suggest you join him. No offense, Maddie, I know this has been a hard day, but I really don't know what you hoped to accomplish by chasing us up here.

FRANK

What we hoped to accomplish was dragging your friend there from behind my limo on a dog chain through the whole state of Texas, back to Fort Worth where he is going to marry my daughter!

TOMMY

Well, when you put it that way, it just sounds so heartfelt and forgiving, and not at all like the rants of a cartoonish, gun-toting Yosemite Sam.

RAY

(Butting in.)

Now, it seems to me the only people not talking about
this very serious subject are the people it affects most.
Reggie, would you agree?

REGGIE

I was just enjoying the exchange.
(Chuckles, some of the other guys laugh as well.)

MADDIE

You're making jokes?
(To the gallery.)
You can laugh at this? You told me you loved me. I
didn't propose to you, you know? I didn't get down on
my knee, tell you I loved you more than anything else
in the world, and place a ring on your finger. That was
you. I thought you were the one I was going to spend
the rest of my life with, and then you do this to me.
Why? Can you at least tell me why?
(To the gallery. Angry now.)
Don't I at least deserve that?

REGGIE

I am really sorry, Madeline. I know I could say that
everyday for the next twenty years and never come
close to making up for what's happened. I know that.
But I still think I made the right decision. I don't think
I'm ready to get married…if I'll ever be ready to get
married. I like my life the way it is, and I loved the fact
that you were part of it, and a great part of it. But the
permanence of marriage is something I'm too
temporary to grasp. And the fact that I was able to
walk out of the ceremony today, effectively solidifying
my position in the hearts and minds of several people I
care about as the biggest asshole on the face of the
planet…Can I use "asshole?"

RAY

It seems to fit here.

REGGIE

Thank you. The fact that I was willing to make myself
look so cowardly in front of those people in order to

avoid what I think to be a life-altering mistake, ought to be a sign of my dedication to my decision…which is that getting married right now would be a huge mistake. And the fact that that's what you want, and not what I want…I figure that signals the end of our relationship. That and the fact that I humiliated you in front of all your loved ones. Did you really come all this way to bring me back, either by dog leash or other method? Do you still want to marry me, even after my obvious disdain for the idea?

MADDIE

Yes, I still want to marry you. Because I know you. You think I wanted to marry a stranger? I know about your insecurities, particularly concerning ideas and concepts of great importance. That childlike insecurity is part of your charm. It's part of what made me fall in love with you. Granted, I never figured it would manifest itself to this extreme, but I thought about that on the way up, and despite my initial reaction upon seeing you, which I'll admit was a little bitchy…Can I use "bitchy?"

TOMMY

It seems to fit here.

MADDIE

(She shoots a mean glance at TOMMY)
Now that I've had a chance to calm down. I still see the man I want to marry. People get worked up over the decisions they have to make, and different people react to those different decisions in different ways.
(Eyeballing TOMMY)
And some people have help in making their decisions that perhaps does not come from the right sources.
(Back to REGGIE)
You think you're the first groom to get cold feet? And do you think I didn't have certain reservations of my own? Of course I did, you just reacted poorly. I'm giving you a mulligan this time, and asking you to

please, realize that you do in fact love me and come
back to Fort Worth with us, and let us start our lives
together as insecure husband and insecure wife.

REGGIE

(Looking deeply into her eyes.)

I always love it when you use golf terminology. So
even after this…cat-and-mouse game through the state
of Texas, you still want to walk down the aisle…and
be with me?

*(MADDIE nods her head, doting over REGGIE,
TOMMY sees REGGIE's resolve breaking down, and
therefore his whole world breaking down with it. He
storms in between MADDIE and REGGIE, looking
scared an angry.)*

TOMMY

No. No!

(To REGGIE)

Don't you see what she's doing? What they're doing?
It's the old "Good cop, Bad cop," with a spin on it that
sends you to a prison of a different kind. You think I'm
going to stand by and just watch it happen?

FRANK

Thomas, stay out of this!

TOMMY

Oh, no, Frank, I'm neck deep in this!

(To MADDIE)

You think you "know" him? You only see the things
he chooses to show you, as do all men with women,
but you think you really know him? That's just funny.
Did he ever tell you how he stole over four-hundred
dollars from the collection plates at his church when he
was fifteen, over the span of two months?

REGGIE

Tommy!

TOMMY

No, he didn't, did he? Or how we cheated on
practically every test all through college, but right

275

before graduation he almost turned himself in to the
Dean after a massive guilt-attack? No, he didn't! I had
to talk him down, you know! Me! I was there for him
when he needed me, and he was a fucking mess! He
was crying, afraid he had shamed his family, and was
receiving a degree under false pretences and all this
other moralistic crap…but you didn't know that either,
did you? Because he didn't let you into that part of his
world, but I've been there the whole time! And you
think I'm just going to stand here and let you try to
take him away from me? You think I'm going back
down to Fort Worth, after the hell I've already gone
through on this trip? Bouncing to and from the most
insignificant cities in a barren landscape, listening to
the points of view of people I could give two shits
about, making myself physically sick, all to try and
deny something about myself that I should have
accepted long ago. I wasn't afraid this whole trip that
Reg was going to marry you and be miserable. I was
afraid he would marry you and I would be miserable!
Because he's mine, you understand? I found him first!
I'm the one that knows him, and I'm the one that loves
him!
*(He grabs REGGIE and kisses him, a kiss of forbidden
love, whatever that is. I guess just a long kiss.)*
*(REGGIE is just plain flabbergasted, surprised and
shocked. So is everyone in the gallery.)*
TOMMY
And if he looked inward deep enough, and accepted
his true feelings, without any hang-ups about
perceptions, or social ramifications or anything else,
I'm sure he'd see what has truly been going on
between us the whole time we've known each other.
MADDIE
Reggie, is this true?
*(REGGIE takes a long time to answer the question.
Thinking. Shocked and thinking.)*

REGGIE

I'm afraid so. I guess the true reason I ran out on you
at the church today isn't because I was afraid of
spending the rest of my life with just one person. It
was because I had already found that one person, and it
just wasn't you. All the plans I've made in my head
concerning my future have had Tommy in them, but
I've always been in denial about the real reason behind
it.

(He walks up to MADDIE and takes her hand.)
Madeline, I'm a homosexual, and I'm in love with
Tommy.

*(MADDIE throws herself into a violent rage, leaps on
top of REGGIE, strangling him and screaming.)*
MADDIE

You piece of shit, I can't believe you would do this to
me! You fuckin' prick! You haven't humiliated me
enough, you fuck?

TOMMY

Maddie, please! It's not his fault!
*(He goes behind her to pull her off, but FRANK pulls
TOMMY off of her.)*
FRANK

Hands off my daughter, faggot!
*(FRANK punches TOMMY in his other eye. TOMMY
reels back, and FRANK joins his daughter in
strangling REGGIE.)*
TOMMY
(To RAY.)

Ray, you've gotta stop this!
RAY

What the fuck can I do? This woman's husband just
left her on her wedding day for another man! It's
fuckin' pandemonium!

*(BILLY RAY and CLETUS finally pull FRANK and
MADDIE off of REGGIE, who's in considerable pain*

but is not angry. He feels deep remorse for hurting
MADDIE in this way.)
FRANK
(Shrugging off CLETUS and BILLY RAY.)
Alright, I'm alright! I'm calm!
(To REGGIE)
You're a dead man, asshole! You're dead! Financially,
I am going to break you! I can legally make you
responsible for all wedding expenses, you know that? I
can probably even get you indicted for fraud, I know
judges in this state, boy! When I'm through with you
you'll wish you'd never met me, princess!
REGGIE
(Still very humbled.)
Sir, I completely understand that and I can't fault you
for your anger. When I explain my choice of lifestyle
to the papers and the news stations, I'll accept full
responsibility.
FRANK
What?
REGGIE
You know, when the society columns ask what made
me switch from women to men, I'll say that I was
simply whisked away by my own immaturity. You
know how they like to write gossip pieces about the
wealthy, but I'm sure they won't draw any conclusions
about your little girl.
MADDIE
Daddy…
REGGIE
And social circles will probably only talk about it for
maybe a year. After that it will be old news, and people
will only say sparingly, "Oh, look, there's Maddie
James, didn't she turn a man gay once?"
FRANK
You think you can scare…

MADDIE

No, daddy, please. Please don't! I just want this to go
away! Please! I can live with people's assumptions that
Reggie left me for another woman, but if this gets out
I'll be the laughing stock of the state of Texas!

FRANK

Honey, this concerns quite a bit of money…

MADDIE

Daddy!

FRANK

(Anger building, but resolve breaking down.)
Alright. Alright, baby girl. Whatever you say.
(To REGGIE.)
You'd better steer clear of Texas for a while, boy.
That's all I got to say about that. Come on, Madeline.
Let's get out of this shithole. I didn't know it was one
of "those" bars.
(He turns to go, then turns back to TOMMY.)
Take him, and choke on him. You two deserve each
other.
(And he spits on the ground.)
(As FRANK turns and walks out the door. MADDIE
walks slowly behind him. FRANK is gone, but
REGGIE stops MADDIE as she walks out the door.)

REGGIE

Maddie, are you going to be alright?

MADDIE

(Wiping away tears.)
I don't know. I guess so.
(She looks at him. Then kisses him.)
I'll miss you.
(To TOMMY)
Take care of him, will ya?

TOMMY

I will.
(She leaves. REGGIE is at the front door as he watches
the limo drive away.)

(REGGIE keeps his head slunk against the door. Then his remorse turns to jubilation. He laughs and starts pointing at TOMMY.)

REGGIE

You are brilliant, my friend! Fucking brilliant! What we did here, pure genius!

TOMMY

(Happy as well, but not sure of what's going on.)
What? What'd I do?

REGGIE

I would have never thought of that. I didn't know what I was thinking, I almost had to go back down to Fort Worth with her! I didn't have any ideas of any way out. But then, in walks old reliable! "We're gay!" he shouts. That came out of nowhere. And then with the big smack on the lips, which I personally thought was a great selling point. I'm not sure I like you telling everybody about my stealing from my church, though.

TOMMY

(Looking down, getting the gist.)

Oh.

REGGIE

(Still jubilant, not noticing TOMMY's dismay.)
I still didn't know where you were going with the whole thing until you said it. "Social ramifications." As soon as you said it I picked up the cue and rolled with it. You knew that a man like Frank James would never let his daughter be humiliated, and you knew the way to humiliate her even more than what I did. A society as shallow as theirs, she'd be crushed if her social circles found out she was converting heterosexual men.

RAY

(Getting it too.)
You mean you two aren't really…
(TOMMY is still looking mopey.)

REGGIE

Hey, Ray, we normally don't dress this well, alright.
We don't have enough fashion sense to be gay. And as
far as putting a room together, forget about it.

*(He laughs more and more at his little jokes. TOMMY
still isn't laughing.)*

And did you see how I picked up on your cues? Jesus,
that was great. It was just like back in college! I felt
alive again! I had new blood running through me...

(Notices TOMMY's lack of expression.)

Hey, come on. I know it was a close one, but it's over
now. You did good. What's the matter?

TOMMY

It's just...It just got so close, I was scared for a minute
there. I thought you were trapped and were gonna get
married two feet in front of a shotgun.

REGGIE

It might have turned out that way if you hadn't gotten
my back. This was great, Tommy! This was above and
beyond. I was really impressed.

TOMMY

(Pretending to be happy.)

Well, I'm not a professional, but...

REGGIE

Gentlemen, please raise your glasses once again.

(Nobody does.)

To the two greatest actors in...where are we again?

RAY

Goodnight.

REGGIE

Right. To the two greatest actors in Goodnight, Texas.
Weaving their webs of deceit...

RAY

No, I mean goodnight to you, sir.

REGGIE

What?

RAY

I have no respect for the both of you. Faking homosexuality to get out of telling the truth to a woman who loves you? It's disrespectful to homosexuals to an infinite degree and just plain cowardly to the woman you scorned so badly. I am usually not in the habit of throwing people out of my place…I always like my customers to feel as though this is their second home, that no one judges them…but as for you two, I'd just as soon never see you again. I'm sorry, please leave.

TOMMY

But Ray…

RAY

Please!

REGGIE

(Pause. Making for the door.)

You know, maybe you're right. I won't deny the cowardly aspect of it, but if a better life is begotten through cowardice…I think more people ought to prescribe to it. Let's go Tommy.

TOMMY

Just a second.

(Tosses him the keys.)

Go ahead and start up the car, you can drive the first leg.

(REGGIE walks out the door.)

TOMMY

Ray, you're right. What happened here tonight was a pathetic display, and I was the biggest loser. You talk about cowardice, but when I told that man I loved him, I meant it. I put myself out there in a big way tonight and we all saw the result. Now, I could be honest with my friend and myself and insist on making my declaration of love to this man again, and risk losing him. Or I could play along with the idea that I made up the gay thing and stay with him the rest of my life.

Honesty is important, but happiness trumps it every
time. I apologize for disturbing the evening.
Goodnight.
                            RAY
            (After a pause, solemnly. To ROCKY)
Rocky, you're up.
                    (TOMMY turns to leave.)
Wait, Tommy.
                (TOMMY turns to the bar again.)
You're gonna need this.
*(RAY takes out a handkerchief and puts ice cubes in it.
                    He crushes the ice a bit.)*
    *(ROCKY walks up to the stage. He pulls a piece of
                    paper from out of his pocket.)*
    (TOMMY watches him as he ices his new shiner.)
                            ROCKY
Fellas, I know it has been a crazy night, but the
unpredictability of situations like the one we just saw
draws a parallel to the work I'm here to recite. Any
one of you that knows me, knows about my love for
this work. It's a classic, which makes it an easy choice,
and I think part of what makes it a classic is the
applicability as a metaphor for the journey we mortals
take from birth to death. No matter how many times I
read and dissect the bulk of the work, this last
paragraph keeps surprising me, puzzling me, and is
finally a passage I can always look to for hope. So, to
keep from babbling on here, I'd like to share with you
the closing paragraph from Mark Twain's The
Adventures of Huckleberry Finn.
"Tom's most well, now, and got his bullet around his
neck on a watch-guard for a watch, and is always
seeing what time it is, and so there ain't nothing more
to write about, and I am rotten glad of it, because if I'd
a knowed what a trouble it was to make a book I
wouldn't a tackled it and ain't a-going to no more. But
I reckon I got to light out for the Territory ahead of the

rest, because Aunt Sally she's going to adopt me and civilize me, and I can't stand it. I been there before. Yours truly, Huck Finn."

(TOMMY leaves as this passage ends, and he mouths the last four words in time with ROCKY.)

END SCENE 3
END ACT 2
CURTAIN

<u>Closing Remarks</u>

I think the all-encompassing truth I'm trying to arrive at in all my plays is the necessity of fun. Life is filled with important decisions to make, and if we were to simply focus on the severity of those decisions, we'd lose our minds. The things that keep us sane are the little enthusiasms we have along the way. These are the things in our daily routine that make us smile, and the people with whom we share those smiles. Never let anyone take those little enjoyments from you, because those are the things that keep you young.

I'm done with my little preachy closing remark and would like to follow it with an apology to women. No, not an apology to the women in my various failed relationships, though an apology is definitely in order, but rather an apology to the gender altogether. These plays are written by a man, for men, and there are very limited female roles. The reason is simple: I can't write women. But hey, if I understood women well enough to write them, I wouldn't have to apologize to them so much, now would I?

As to the men folk, I can only say, "Enjoy." These plays were written for you. They have shouting matches, comedic conversations, asinine observations and obnoxious banter…a little something for everyone. Hope to see you on-stage sometime.

Cheers,
JWG

About the Author

Jeremey Gingrich was born in Germany and has lived in many exotic locales since. He's hung his hat in Spain, New Jersey, Virginia, and Canton, Georgia, just to name a few. His family is scattered all about the country as well, with roots in Kentucky, Texas and California. Gingrich spent his college years at the United States Air Force Academy in Colorado Springs and acted as Assistant Coach for their Division 1 College Basketball team following graduation. He is currently an officer in the Air Force, living in Columbia, South Carolina. Jeremey continues to write numerous plays, and the occasional novel, and he is active in community theatre, with acting credits at Columbia's Town Theatre and Workshop Theatre.